To [illegible]

May,

Well Met!
I so enjoyed our time
& Thank you for your
very important & brilliant work!
All Best Blessings,

[illegible]

CARL AUSTIN HYATT

PHOTOGRAPHY

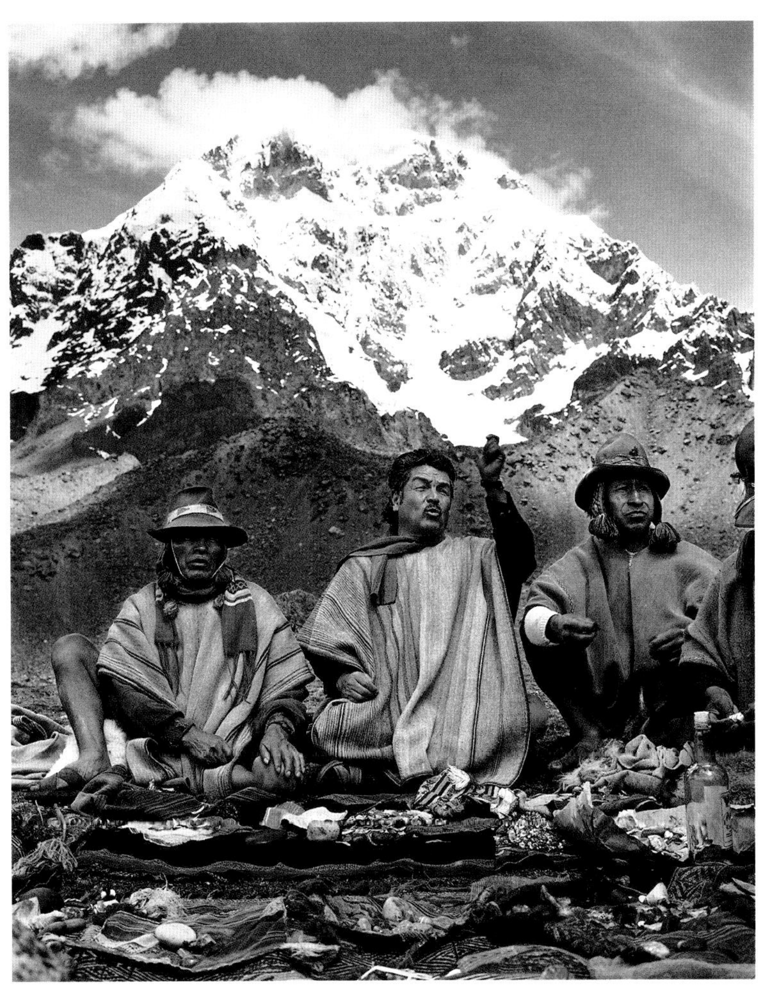

CARL AUSTIN HYATT

PHOTOGRAPHY

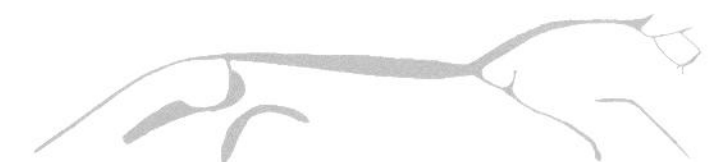

Introduction by Russell Lord
Essay by Tom Crockett

This book is published in conjunction with the exhibition "First Light" held at the New Hampshire INSTITUTE of Art

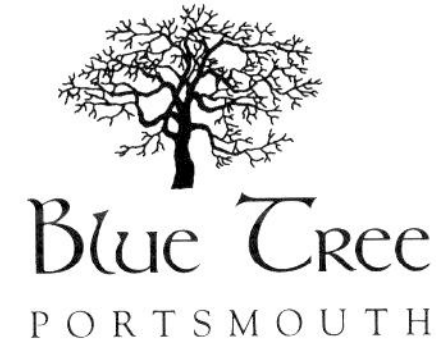

Blue Tree
PORTSMOUTH

First published in the United States in 2007
by Blue Tree, LLC
P.O. Box 148
Portsmouth, NH 03802
www.TheBlueTree.com

37 10 1

Title page: Ceremony at Apu Ausangate, Peru, 2000

Printed in Hong Kong

Carl Austin Hyatt: Photography
Hyatt, Carl A.

ISBN-10: 0-9792014-0-3
ISBN-13: 978-0-9792014-0-0

For customer service and orders:
Local 603.436.0831
Toll-Free 1.866.852.5357
Email sales@TheBlueTree.com

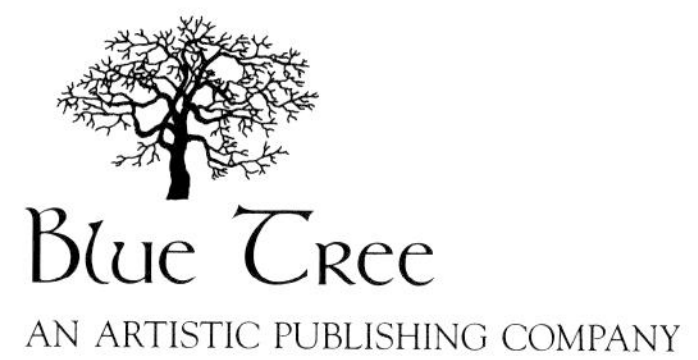

AN ARTISTIC PUBLISHING COMPANY

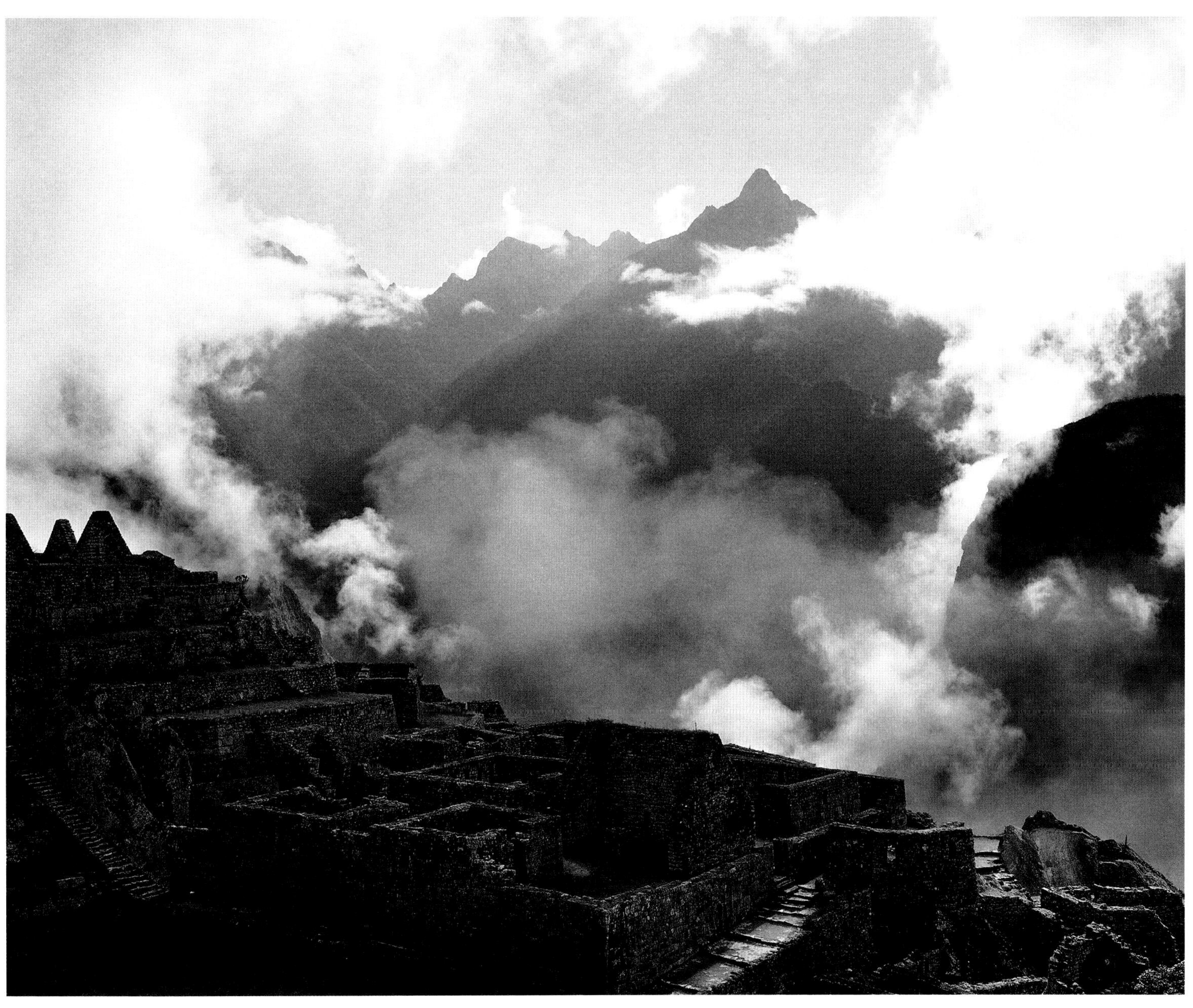

Dawn at Machu Picchu, with Clouds, Peru, 2000

In memory of Marty Elkin.

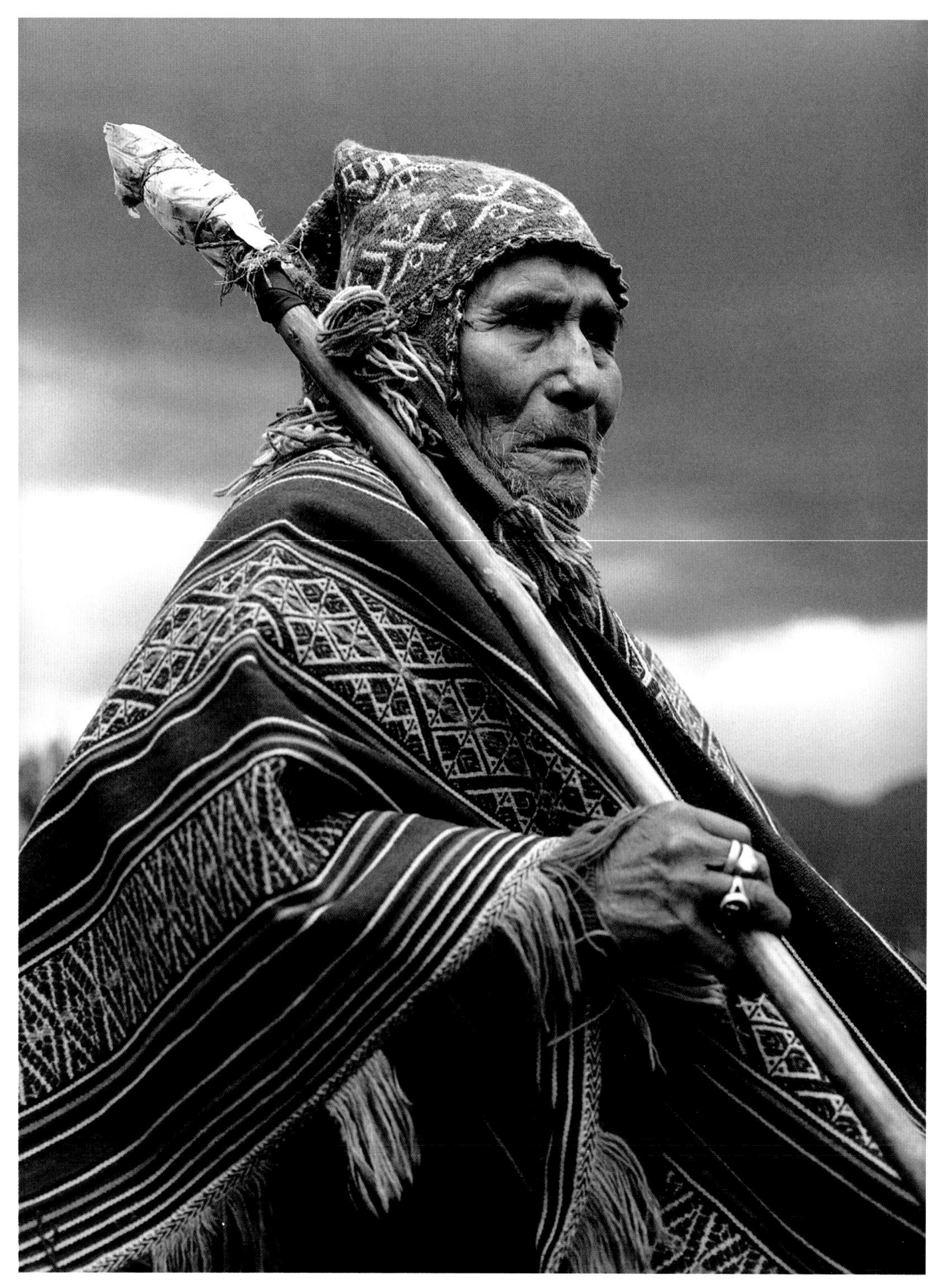

Don Maximo, Cuzco, Peru, 2005

Acknowledgments

For ninety years the New Hampshire Institute of Art has mounted outstanding exhibitions of art for the greater Manchester community. With the introduction of the Bachelor of Fine Arts degree program ten years ago, the exhibition program has grown and expanded. The annual Institute calendar features the work of faculty and of students, selected groups and competitive exhibitions ranging from regional to international in scope, and of course, highly acclaimed artists like Carl Austin Hyatt in one-person exhibitions.

This rich program is an important resource for students in the degree and continuing education and certificate programs. In addition to this critical segment of our audience, viewers throughout the Northeast are regular visitors to the Institute galleries.

We are all extremely grateful to Mr. Hyatt for providing the exhibit to the Institute, and we hope that the galleries properly showcase the work for those who attend. Many people have contributed their professional expertise and labor to make the exhibit possible. First, the project would not exist if Elizabeth Johansson and James Aponovich had not introduced Mr. Hyatt to the Institute, special thanks to them. With this successful beginning, the Institute Exhibition Committee, under the leadership of Patrick McCay, Academic Dean, worked out the many details around logistics and budget. The curatorial judgments of Gary Samson, Chairperson of Photography at the Institute and Kurt Sundstrom, Associate Curator at the Currier Museum of Art, shaped the selection of images that make up the exhibition. Brian Smestad of Blue Tree and Jamie LaFleur of The Banks Gallery have beautifully managed the design and production of this publication. Managing us through this process has been skillfully accomplished by Tricia Rose Burt, Institute Gallery Director. Finally, we appreciate the sponsorship of McLane, Graf, Raulerson & Middleton, P.A.; Ocean National Bank; The Banks Gallery and the Wach Gallery, as well as the operating support provided by the New Hampshire State Council on the Arts.

The images in the exhibition were produced through keen and thoughtful observations and transcend this critical foundation by becoming expressive statements that engage our intellect and heart. We are most appreciative to Mr. Hyatt for providing this outstanding exhibition.

—Roger Williams, President
New Hampshire Institute of Art

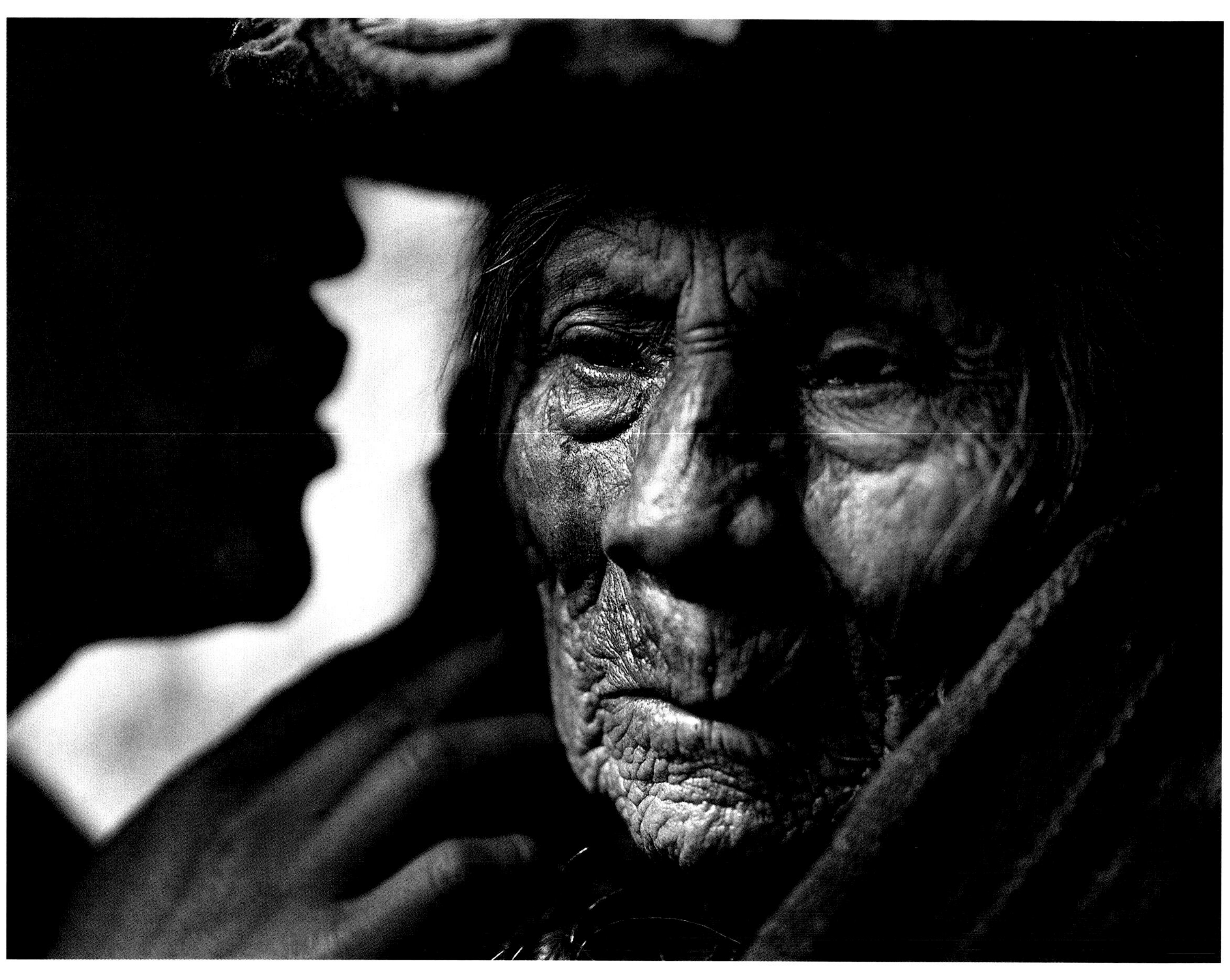

Doña Lucia, Chinchero, Peru 2003

Introduction

Photography is a combination of science and spirituality. In every photograph there is chemistry, that which is quantifiable, measured out in doses and drams. But there is also something ephemeral, the magic of fixing a shadow, a trace of light, or the preservation of a fleeting moment. Carl Austin Hyatt's photographs remind us of the presence of these two seemingly contradictory qualities as he seeks out the spiritual possibilities in natural form be it in the human body or a coastal landscape.

The work presented here could easily be divided into six groups based on subject matter: Peruvian portraits and landscapes, New England coastal landscapes, standing stones, salt piles, nudes, and portraits of women. But photography is a generous medium, and while a camera ostensibly points to a person, place, or thing, it is the ample portions of detail that define the subject in Hyatt's work. Each of his photographs is demanding, forcefully calling our attention to this or that rock, face, surface, curve, cloud, tone, reflection, wrinkle, shadow or skin. In each of these details we begin to recognize a gentle repetition of form in everything, as if to suggest that all life is earth and earth, life. Nature and humanity are unified here as compilations of shapes and textures. Hyatt's discerning eye rests on landscapes that are bodies, bodies that blend into rock, and portraits of people as chiseled as rock or as soft as fine-grained sand. There is a level of intimacy with each subject that shows Hyatt carefully tracing the topography of forms in nature.

The relationship between photography and nature has a long history. One could argue that the first 'photographs' actually occurred naturally in the form of sunburns, faded curtains, or patterns in grassy fields—long before the medium (as we know it) was established in the nineteenth century. Even when a handful of people in the early nineteenth century learned how to capture this phenomenon on chemically treated surfaces, fixing shadows and images, they still spoke of it—with awe—as a product of nature. William Henry Fox Talbot, the inventor of the paper negative process, referred to his discovery as *The Process by Which Natural Objects May Be Made to Delineate Themselves without the Aid of the Artist's Pencil* and poetically titled his photographically illustrated book *The Pencil of Nature*. Hyatt's photographs continue to expand the dialogue on this subject, making explicit the presence of nature in everything, including the photographic process itself.

Light and dark, black and white, negative and positive. Photography is built on oppositions, and Hyatt reminds us that so too is nature. In one shoreline landscape, the snow-covered coast contrasts sharply with the deep wintry dark of the cold, wet rocks exposed to the ebb and flow of the tide. These black and white bands snake along together in a rhythmic dance. Here nature offers us her own negative and positive combination that Hyatt diligently records.

In another, a tidal pool's surface, smoother than silk, reflects the aggressive, jagged edges of the rock jutting out above it. Perhaps this rock has assumed a defensive posture as it continues its constant battle with the sea against its gradual transformation into sand. In yet another, two larger rock formations stretch like thick, muscly arms out into the ocean, guarding the pebbled cove and turning the advancing waves into churning foam made smooth during the exposure time. In all of these pictures, the world is paused; Hyatt gives us a moment to reflect on a landscape in the process of becoming. Indeed, the brief duration of the exposure literally allows us to watch it become.

If the sea is gradually swallowing minerals, we are gradually extracting them from its grasp, as Hyatt's photographs of salt piles point out. Photography is a democratic medium, offering every subject a chance at majesty, and a pile of salt is no exception: here, one masquerades as a mountain or a glacier, slowly and ominously advancing under cover of tempestuous clouds, decorated with richly toned rivulets and crowned with a halo of soft, wispy light. It is a reminder of the awesome destructive and corrosive power of a tiny grain.

Or its creative power, since salt is a key ingredient in many photographic processes from the earliest salt paper prints to Hyatt's platinum prints. These photographs insinuate a rather poetic cycle: salt is born out of water with the power to devour concrete and steel only to be dissolved again and trapped in an image on a slim piece of paper.

Such references to the photographic elements in nature can be found throughout Hyatt's work, dedicated as he is to the transcendent power of the natural world. Rays of sunlight break through the clouds in one seascape to illuminate the peak of a massive rock that spans the foreground. In another the clouds open up to spotlight a distant group of rocks. This streaming light simultaneously illuminates the landscape to dramatic effect and exposes the film in the camera, offering a record of the same momentary scene that has set before us. These are photographs about photography. If these natural objects are being made to delineate themselves then Hyatt is our careful and intelligent guide, in close communication with nature itself.

There is strength, power, and balance in Hyatt's work. In his 'Standing Stone' series, single elongated stones stand upright with purposeful posture surveying the Atlantic. Like ancient stone circles or monuments, they seem primal and raw but also mysterious, suggesting some undiscovered narrative. At times they appear as solid sentinels of the shoreline, elsewhere they remind us of lonely, hopeful figures frozen on their unforgiving "widow's walks," waiting for the return of something. In all cases, these figures appear animated from within, at once active in, as well as a part of, the landscape they inhabit. Hyatt's pictures allow us to glimpse the secret lives of stones.

Just as Edward Weston once said that nature offered an infinite number of perfect 'compositions,' Hyatt's nudes suggest the endless possibilities of the human body Through the simple play of light and shadow on bare skin, delightfully dizzying

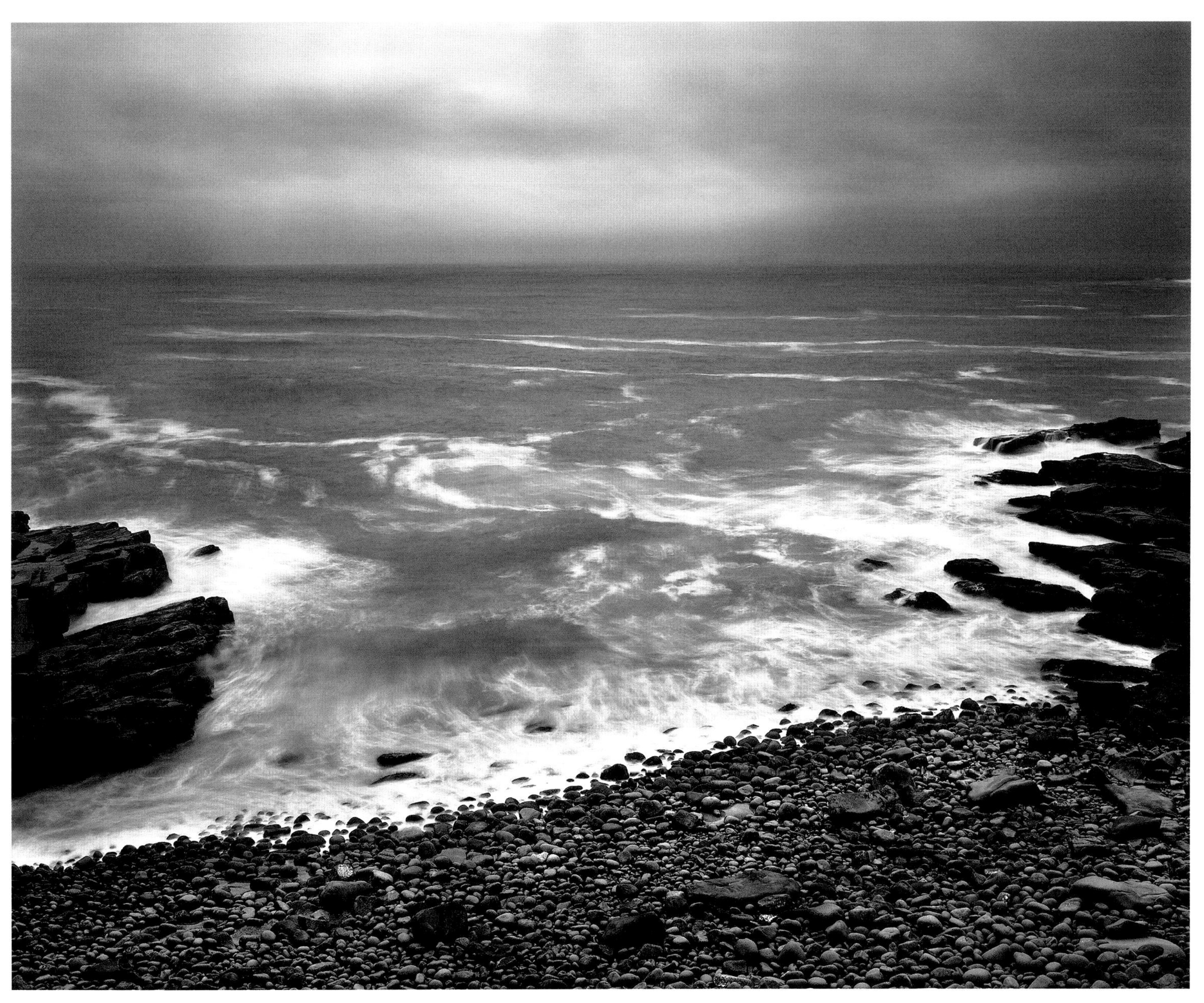

Monument Cove, Acadia National Park, Maine, 1993

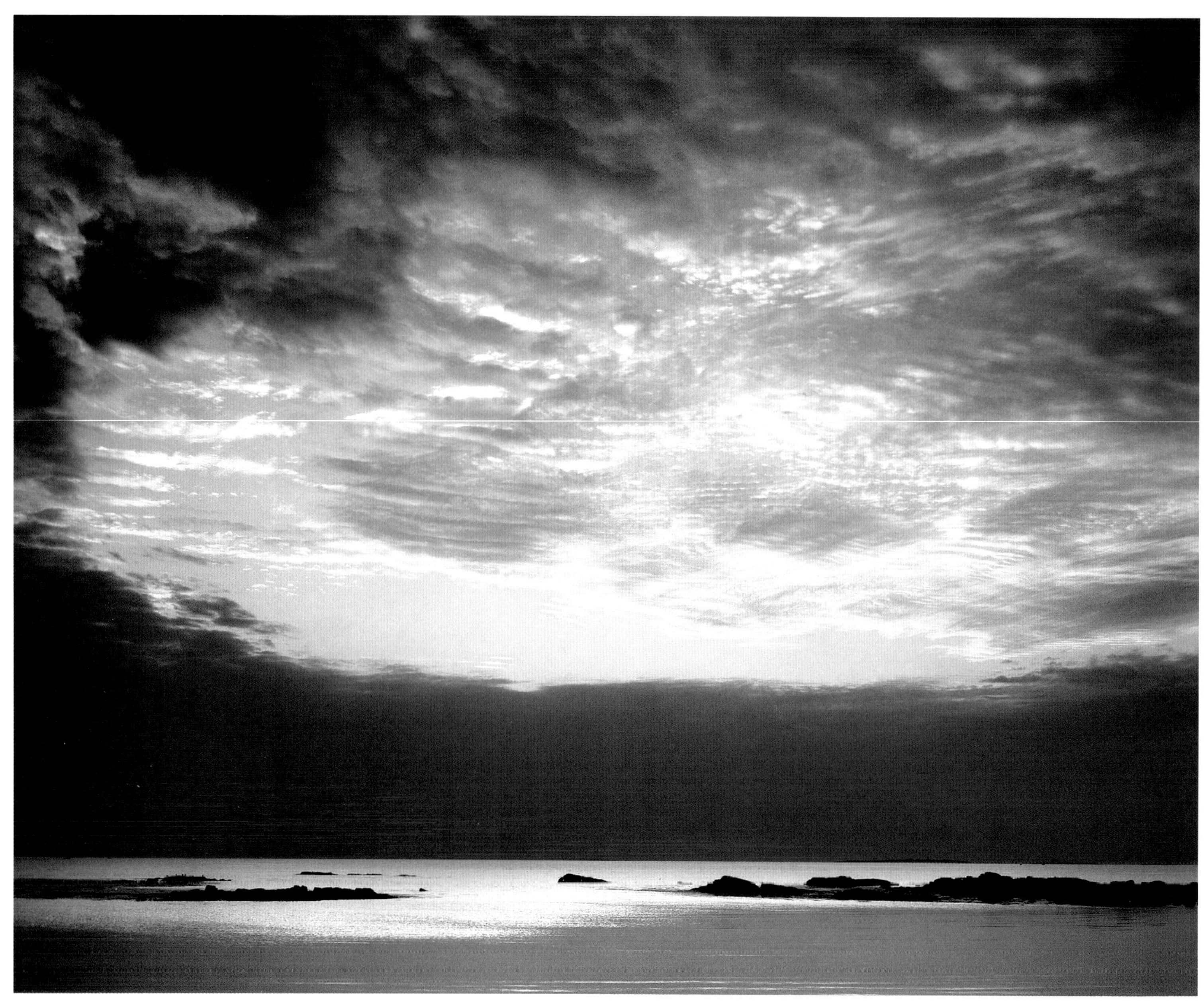

Dawn at Odiorne Point, New Hampshire, 1994

landscapes emerge. In a few pictures Hyatt even juxtaposes body and landscape, showing legs and arms draped over rock just as each sedimentary layer rests on top of another.

There is a striking immediacy to his portraits of women. Through their eyes we find ourselves where Hyatt once stood, with the photograph serving as a window through which we are connected to the subject and the photographer. It is a moment at once past and present.

The book starts with pictures of Peruvian shamans and a view of Machu Picchu, which is perhaps the most appropriate way to begin. Here, among the first pictures, is an image of a whisper between a young man and a blind woman. It is as if a secret is being shared, something ancient, something sacred, something spiritual. Blindness has often been a metaphor for vision of another kind and this woman is the perfect guide for these pictures: they must be felt and not simply seen. Shamans intuitively understand the spiritual in nature and here, seen as monumental guardians of this secret, they introduce us to the rest of Hyatt's work.

In present day thought, informed by centuries of rationalism, science and spirituality are often pitted against each other as enemies. As a result, it is easy to forget how closely aligned and interconnected they are. The raw science of geological metamorphism creates rock and land, while the moon's gravitational pull slowly helps the sea shape the coastline into sculptural landscapes for spiritual contemplation, just as the raw chemistry of the photograph preserves these scenes in simple constructs of light, paper, salt, metal or pigment.

All valid art forms, once discovered continue to exist and persist. Hyatt follows in a rich tradition in photography, but it is, perhaps, the supreme tradition: the search for beauty and truth, far older than photography itself. Hyatt's pictures prove that beauty is, and always has been, all around us and even part of us. And photography is the perfect medium with which to undertake this search, for the process itself wrestles with concepts of objective truth and subjective beauty, with nature and humanity, with chemistry and wonder. In Carl Austin Hyatt's photographs all converge to suggest the beauty and truth in every form and at every scale, from a massive, majestic coastal landscape to a simple grain of salt.

—Russell Lord
PhD Candidate in Art History
The Graduate Center
City University of New York

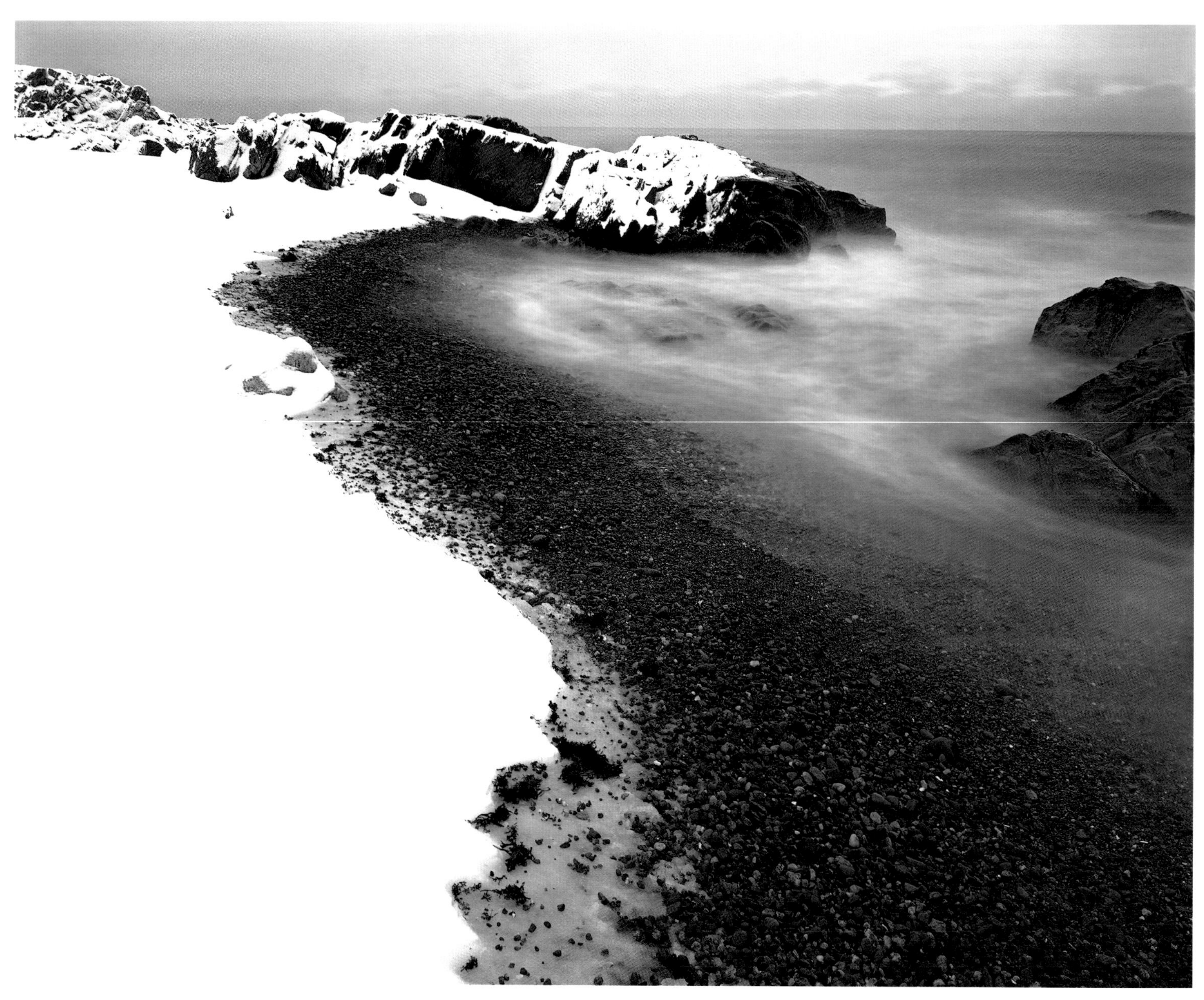

North of Wallis Sands, New Hampshire, 1985

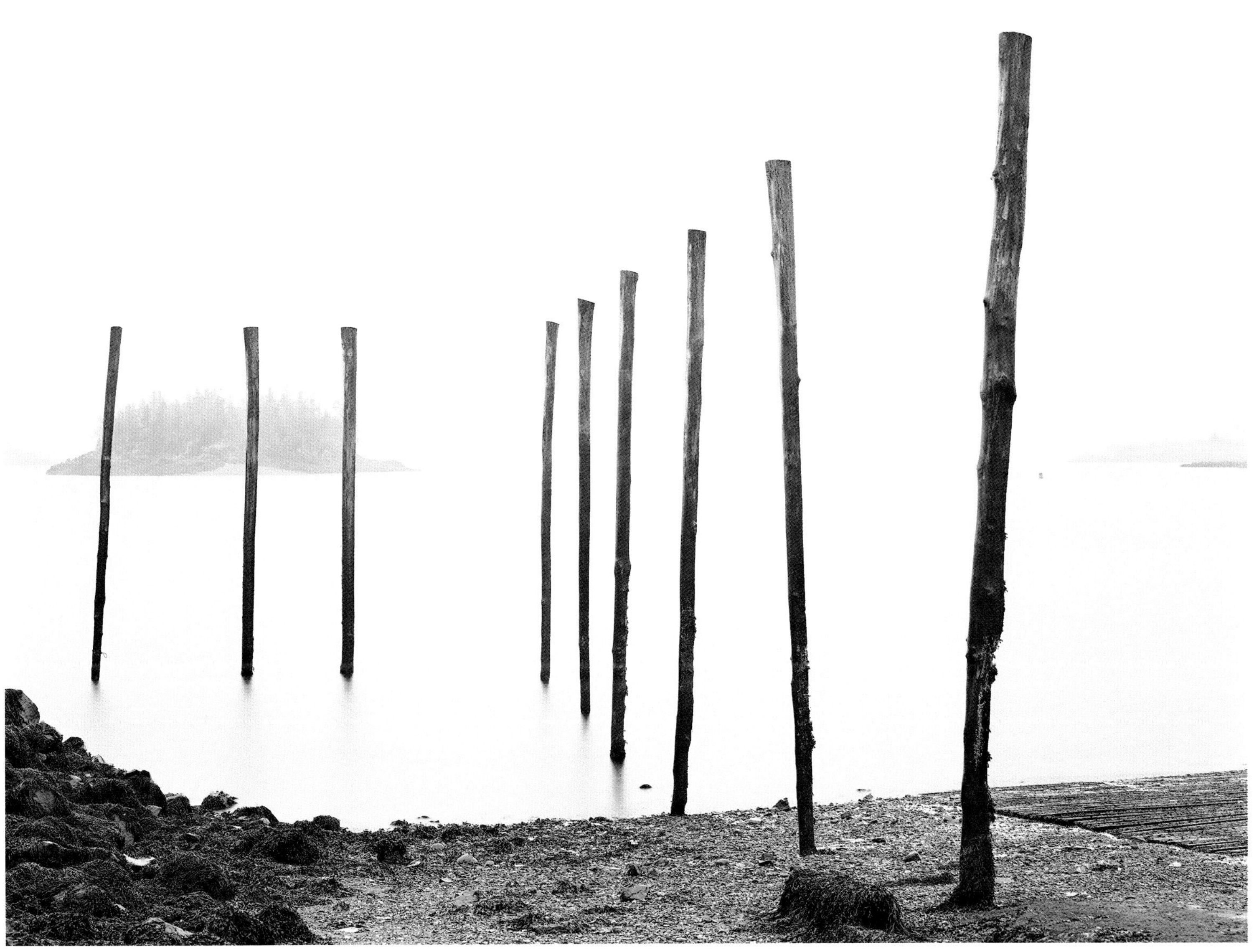

Poles at Lubec, Maine, 1993

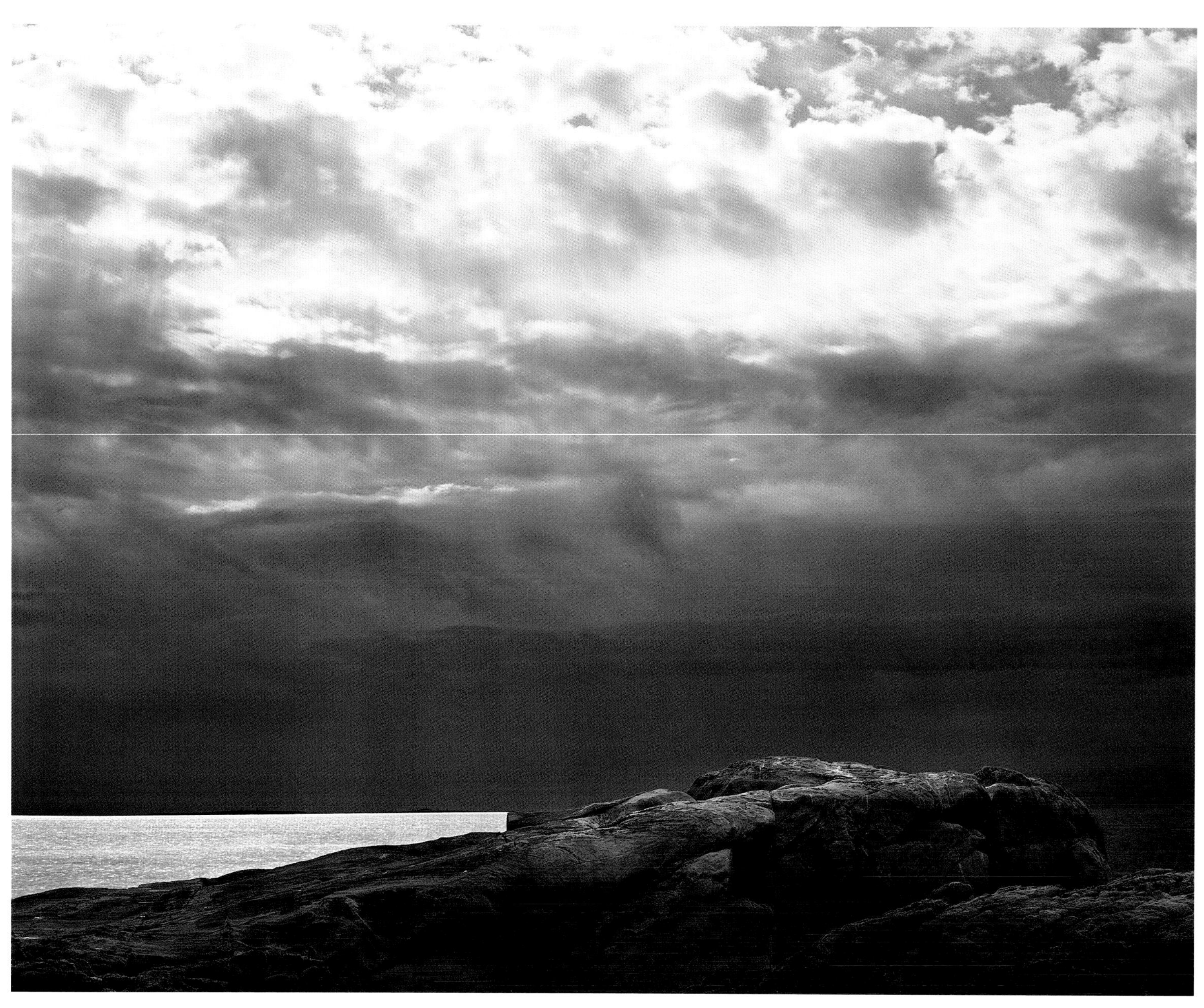

Pulpit Rock, New Hampshire, 1993

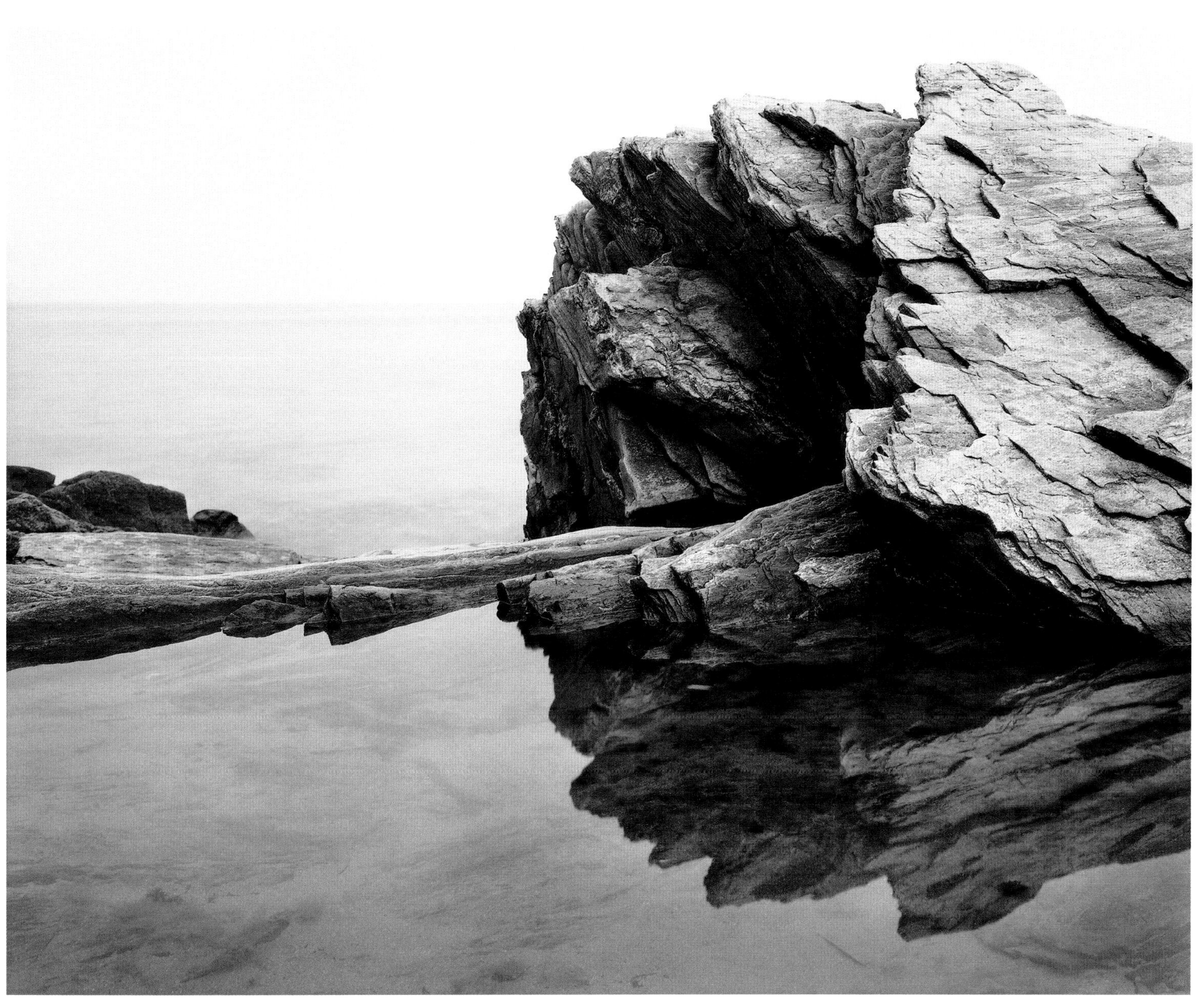

Gray Point, New Hampshire, 1993

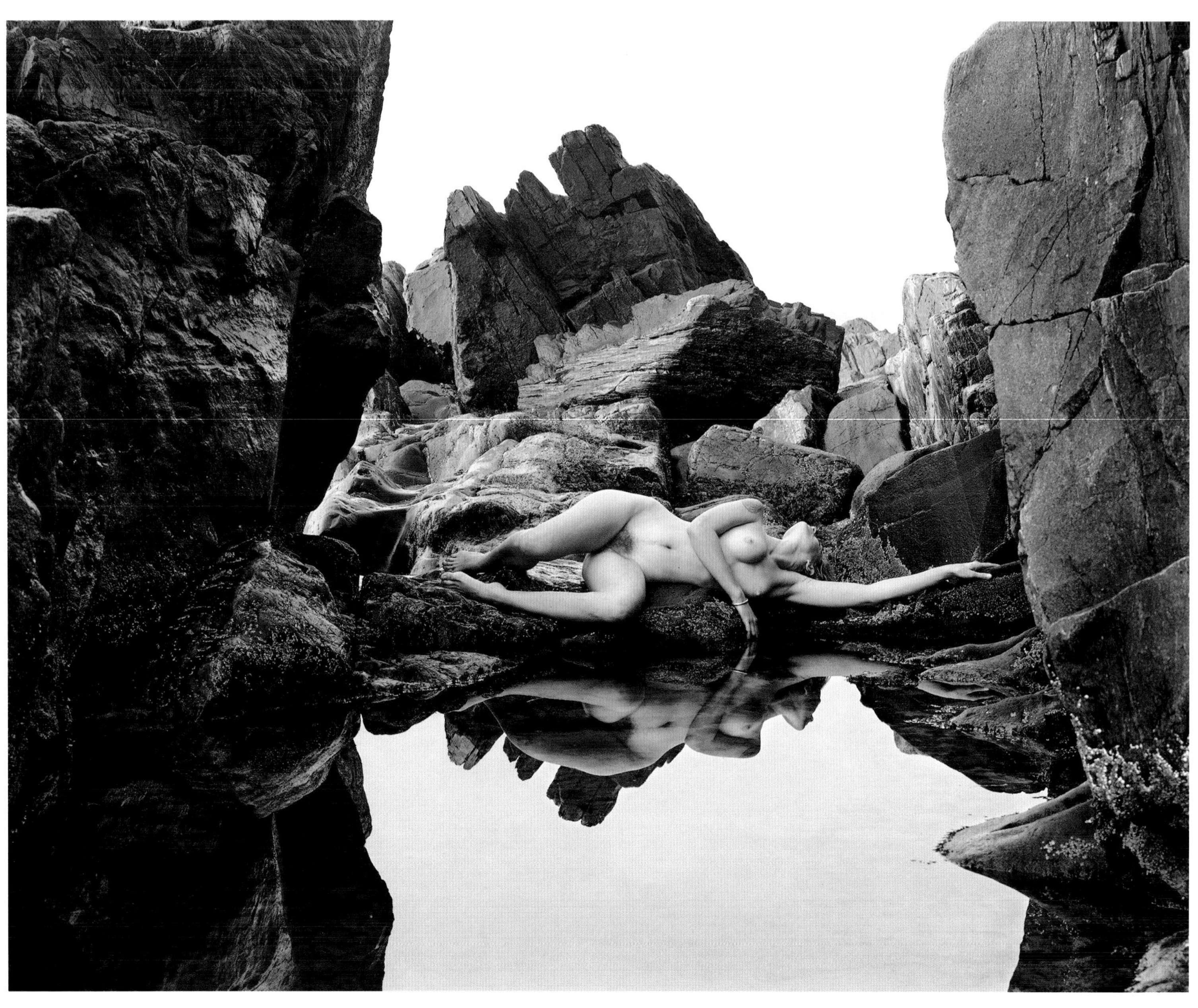

N-101, 1997

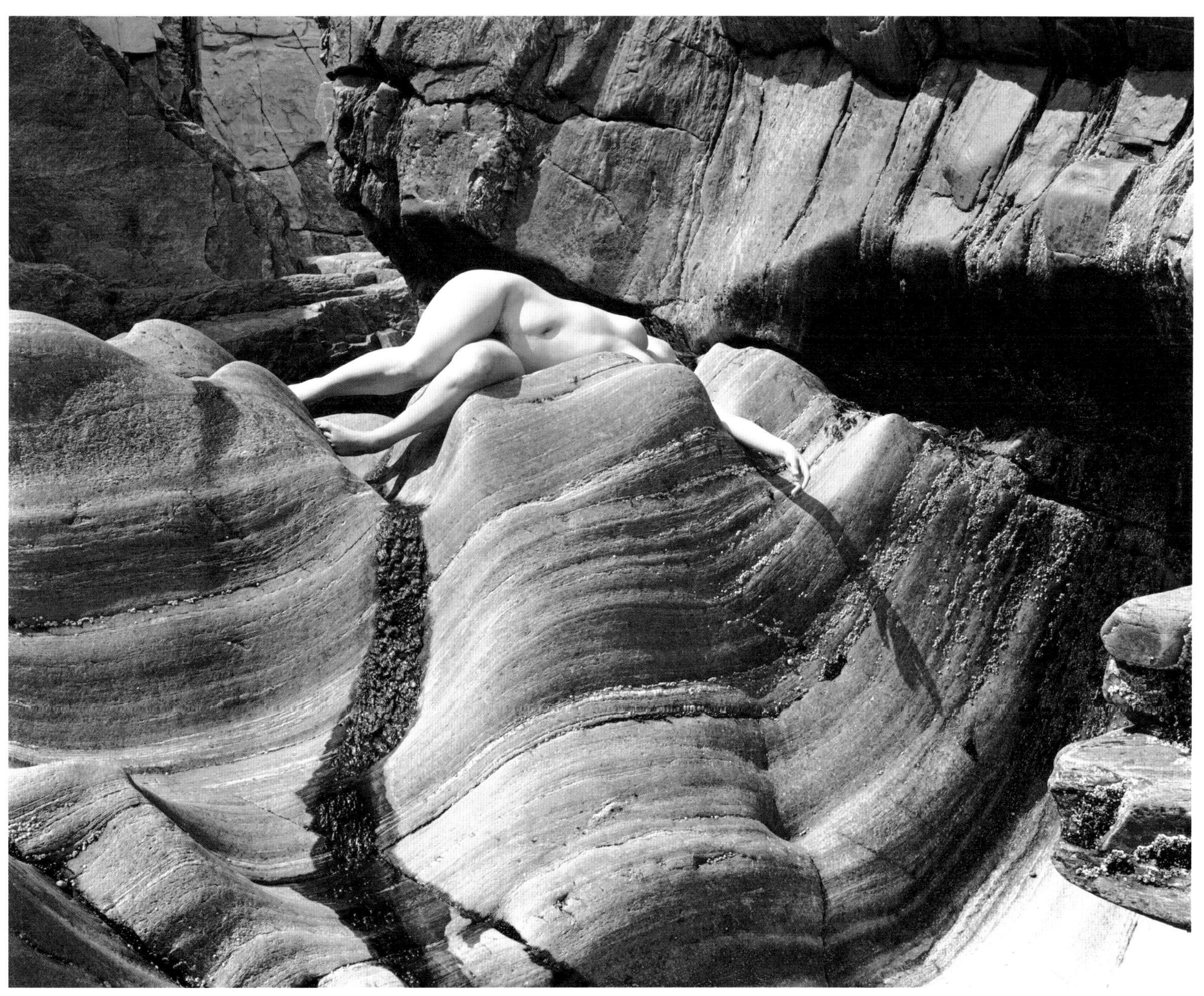

N-173, 2005

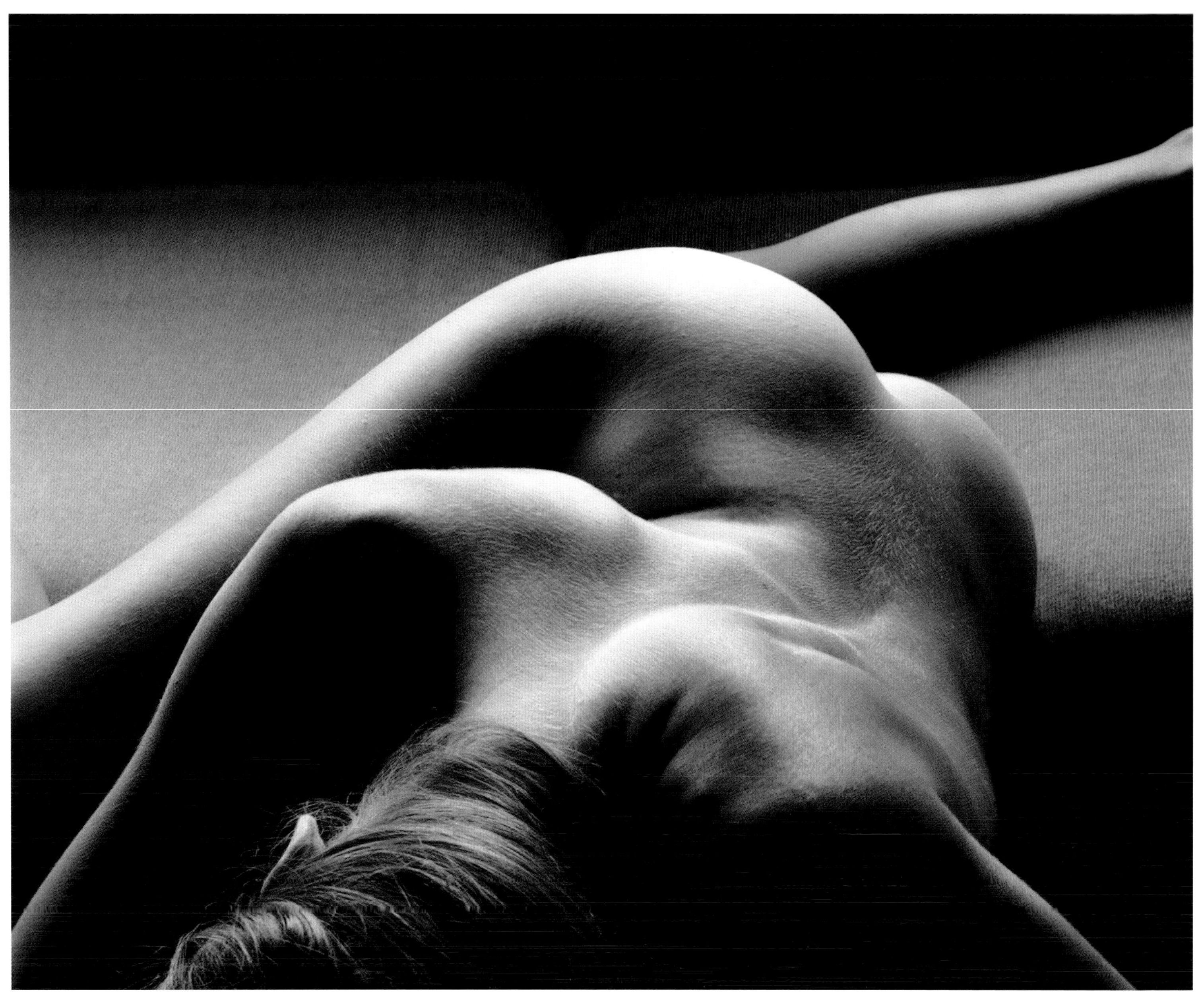

N-1, 1990

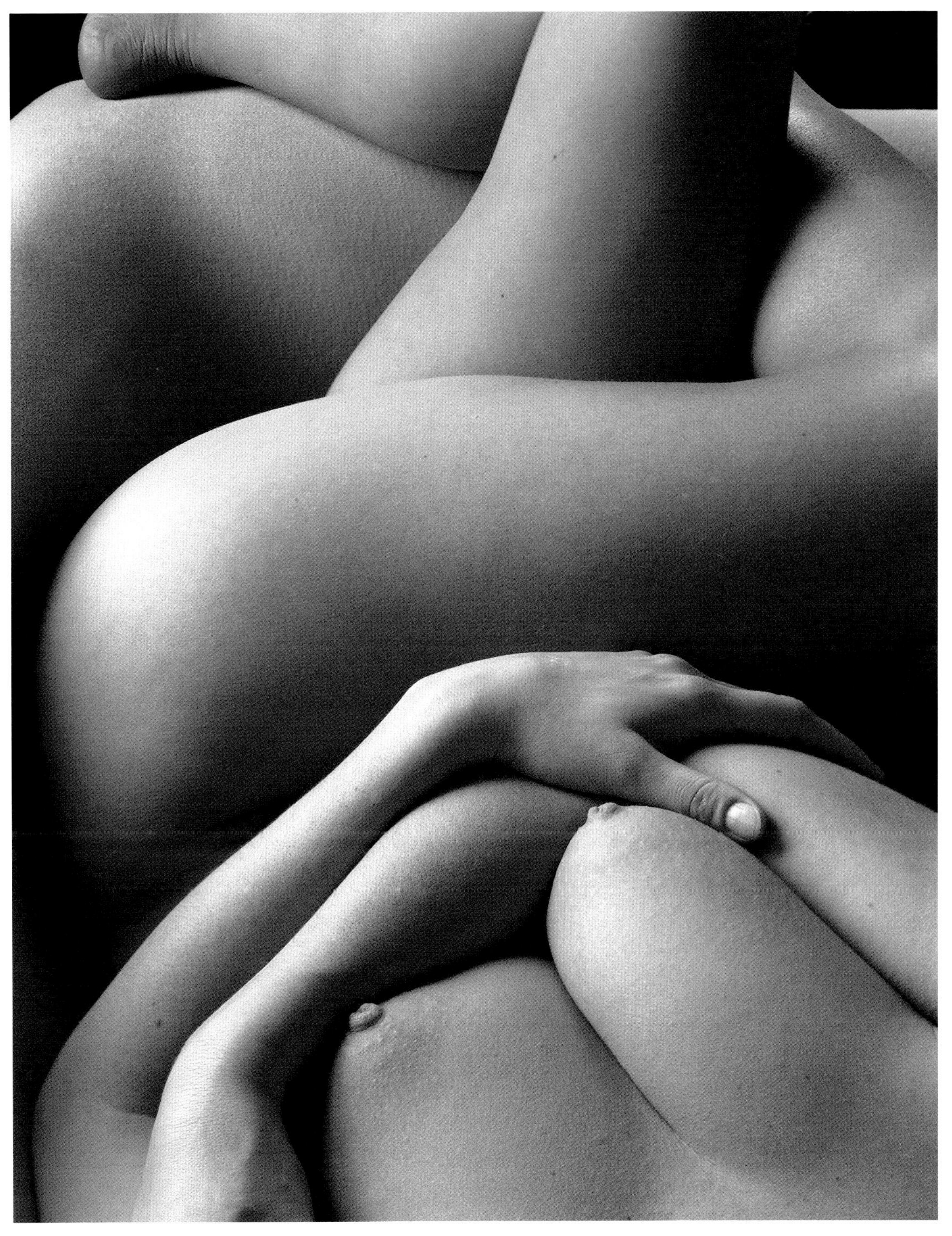

N-71, 1994

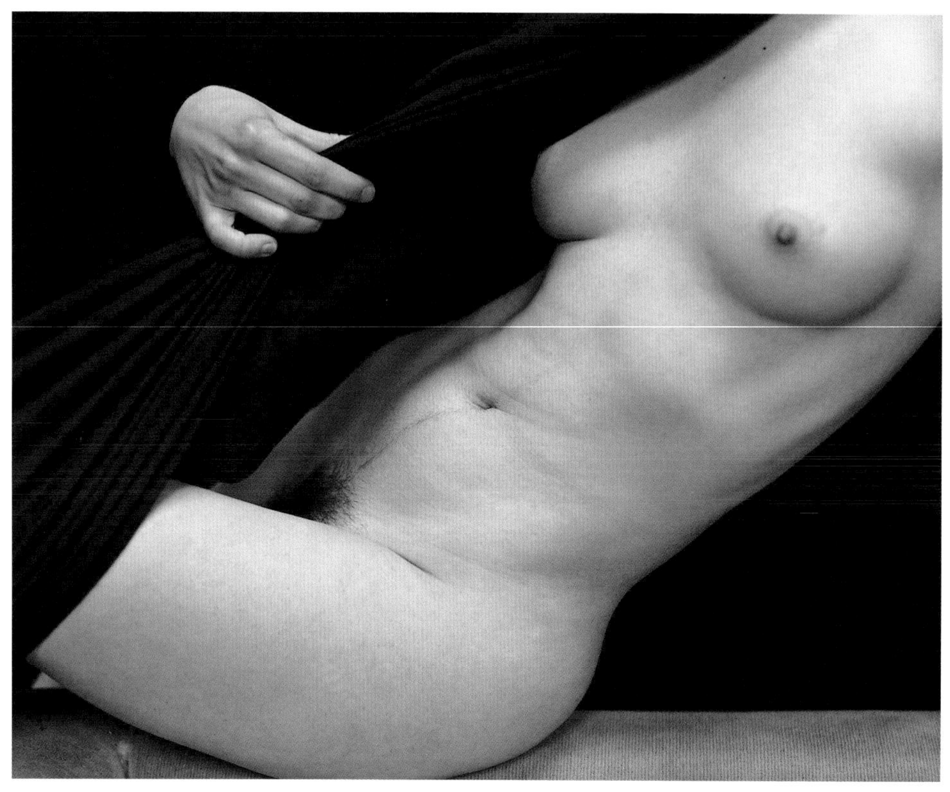

N-78, 1997

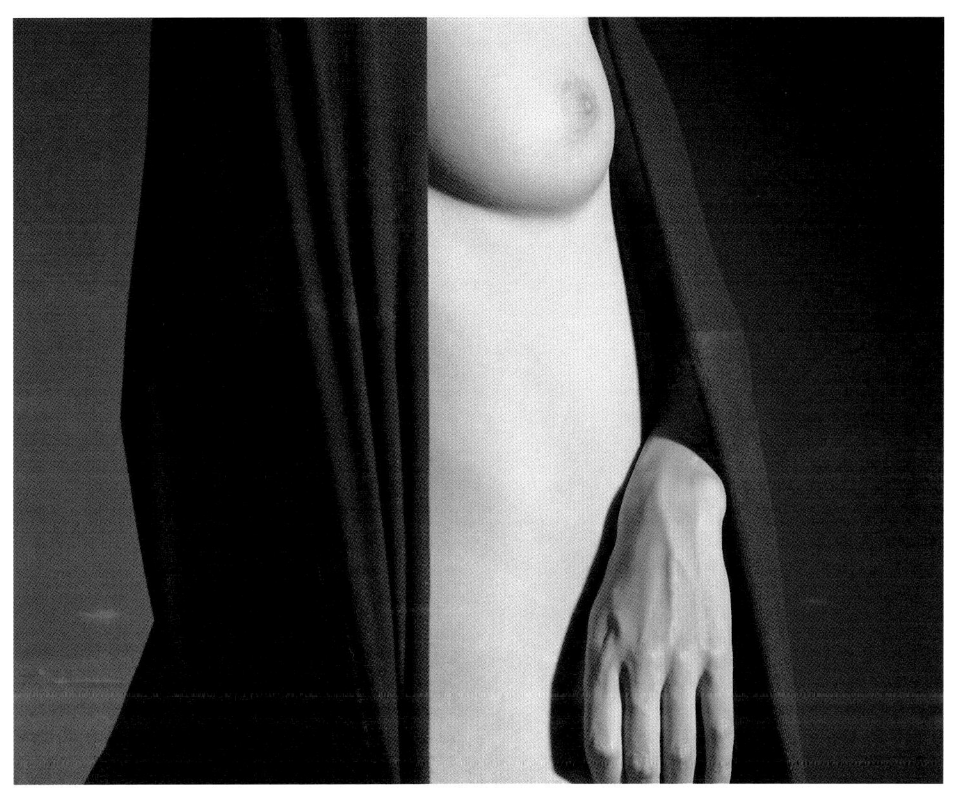

N-23, 1990

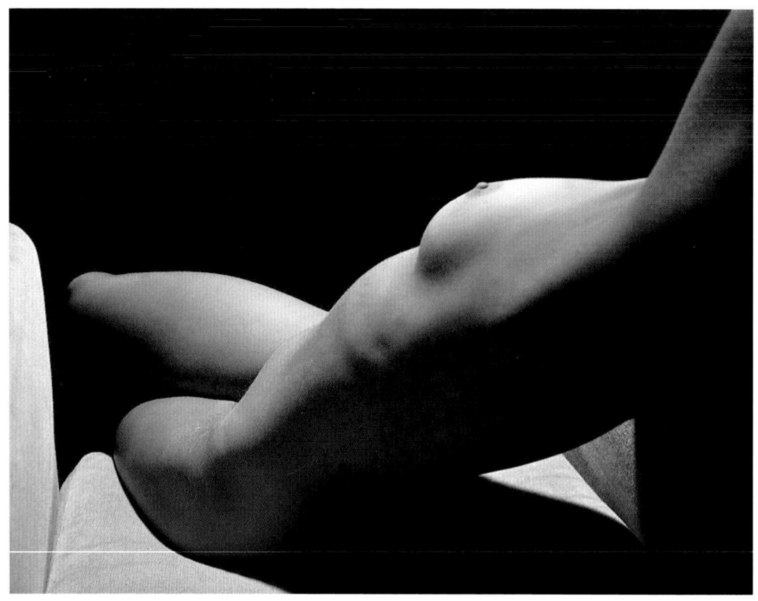

N-16, 1990

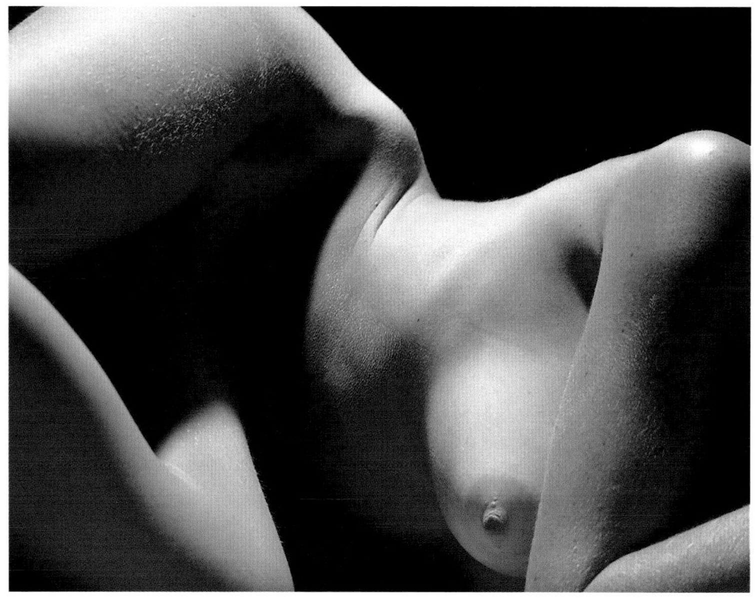

N-15, 1990

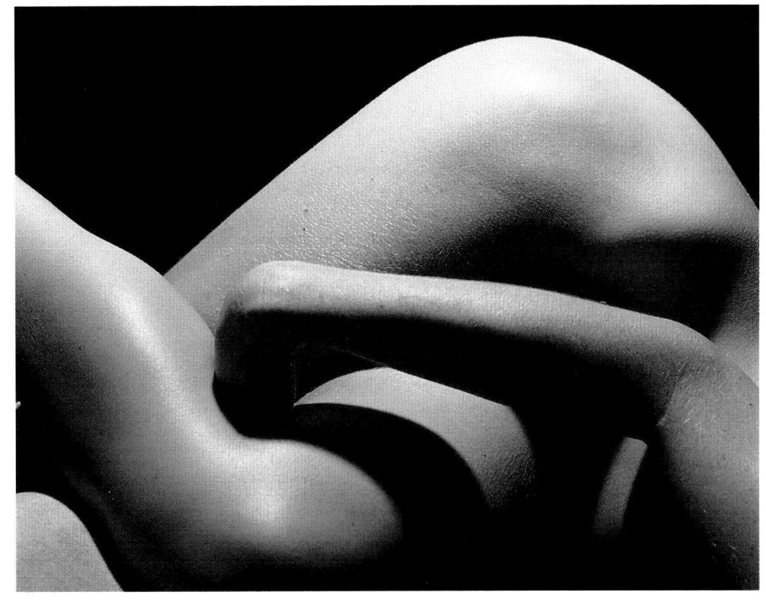

N-14, 1990

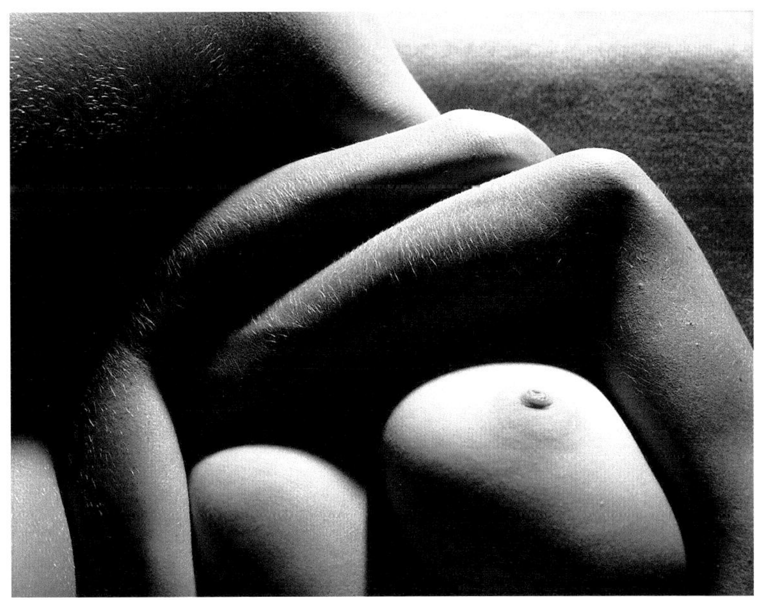

N-17, 1990

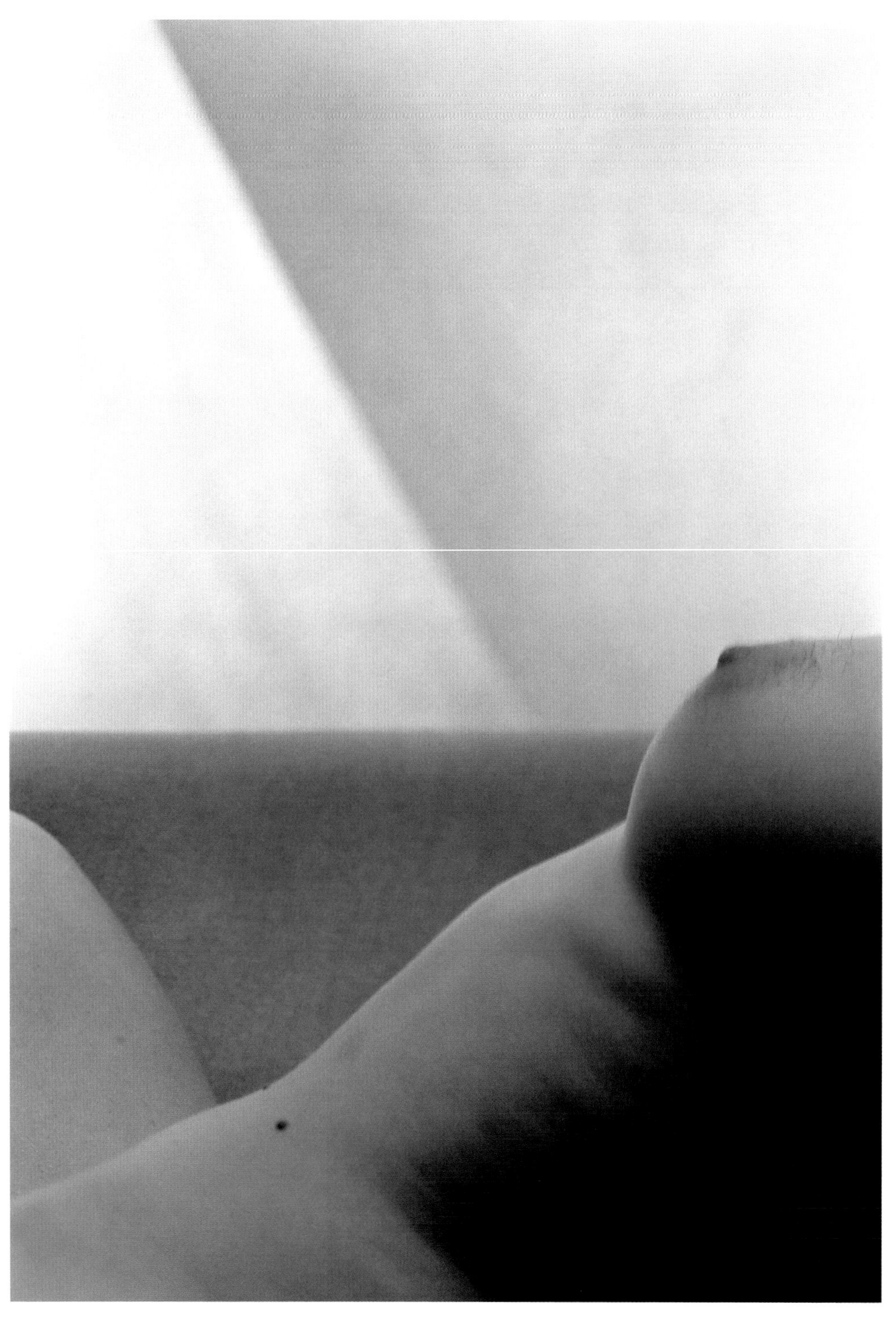

N-119, 1998

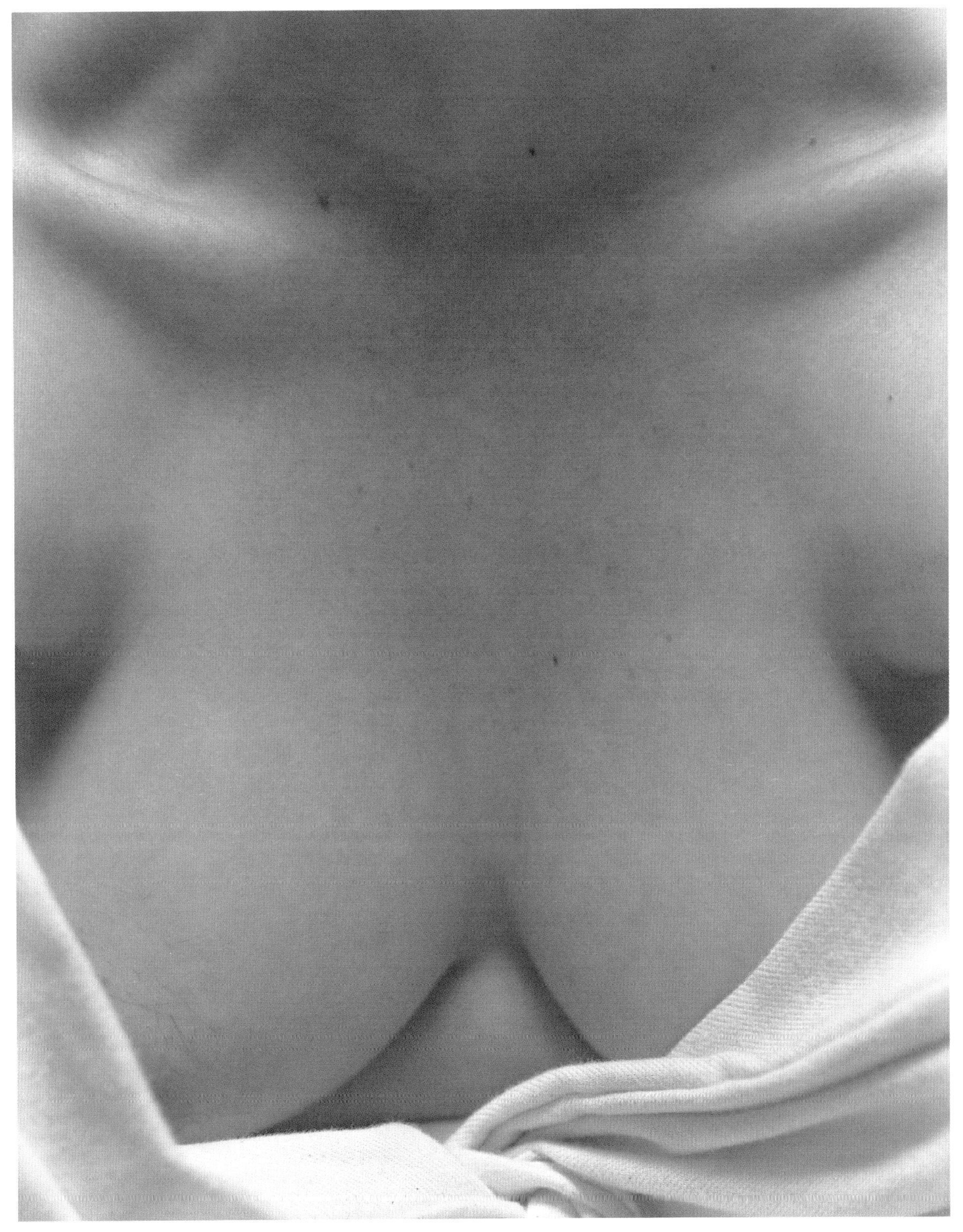

N 110, 1998

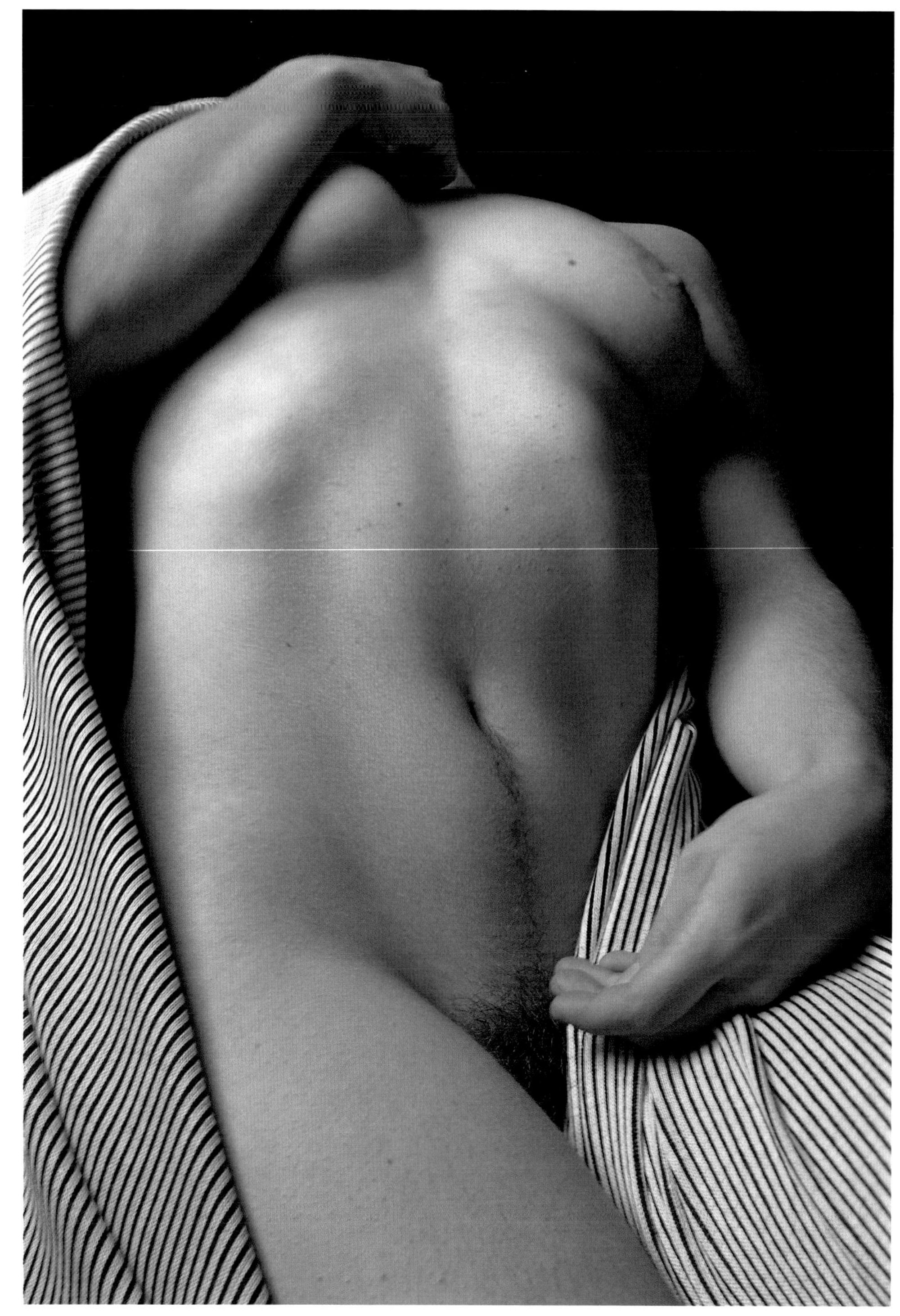

N-10, 1989

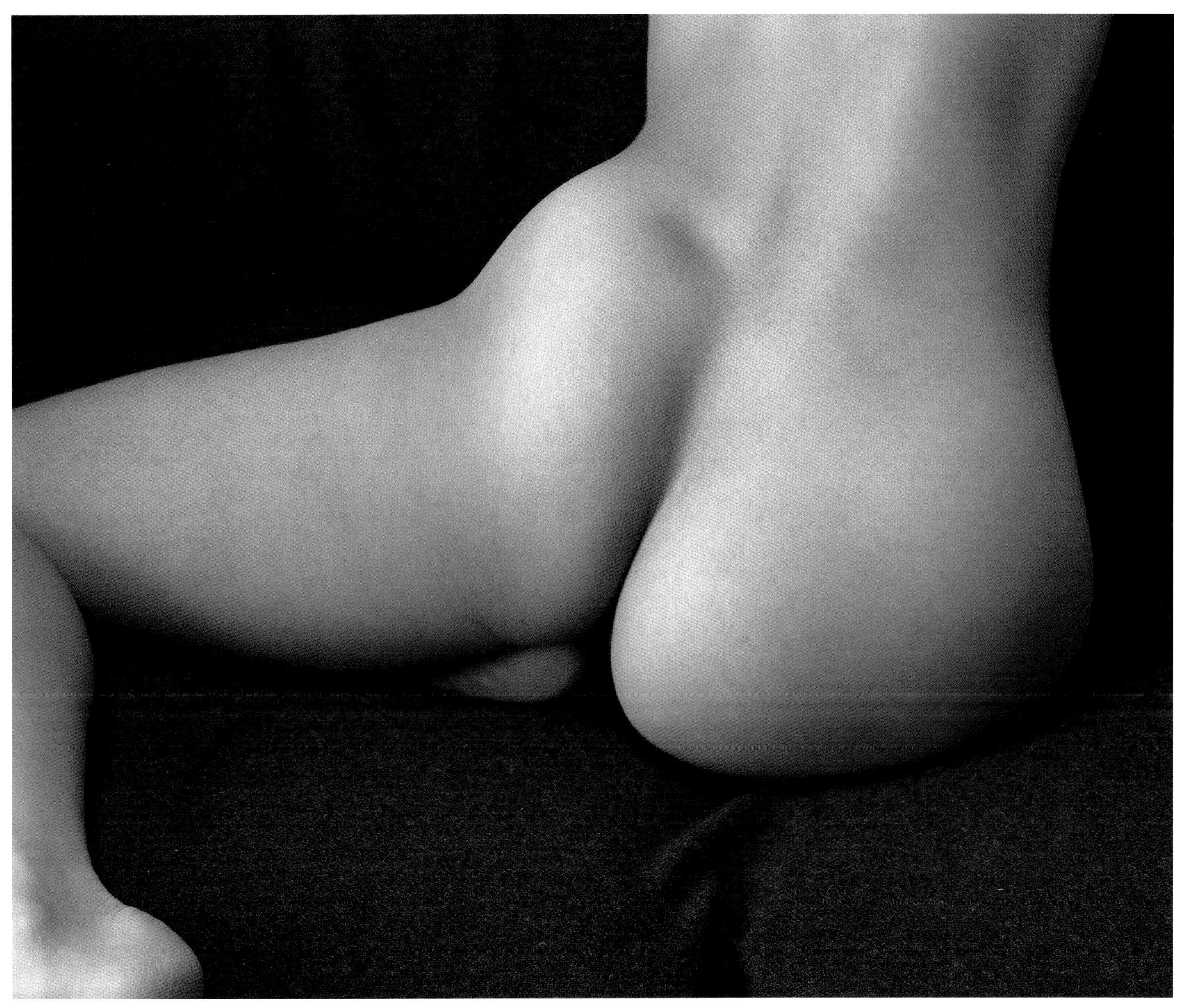

N-82, 1997

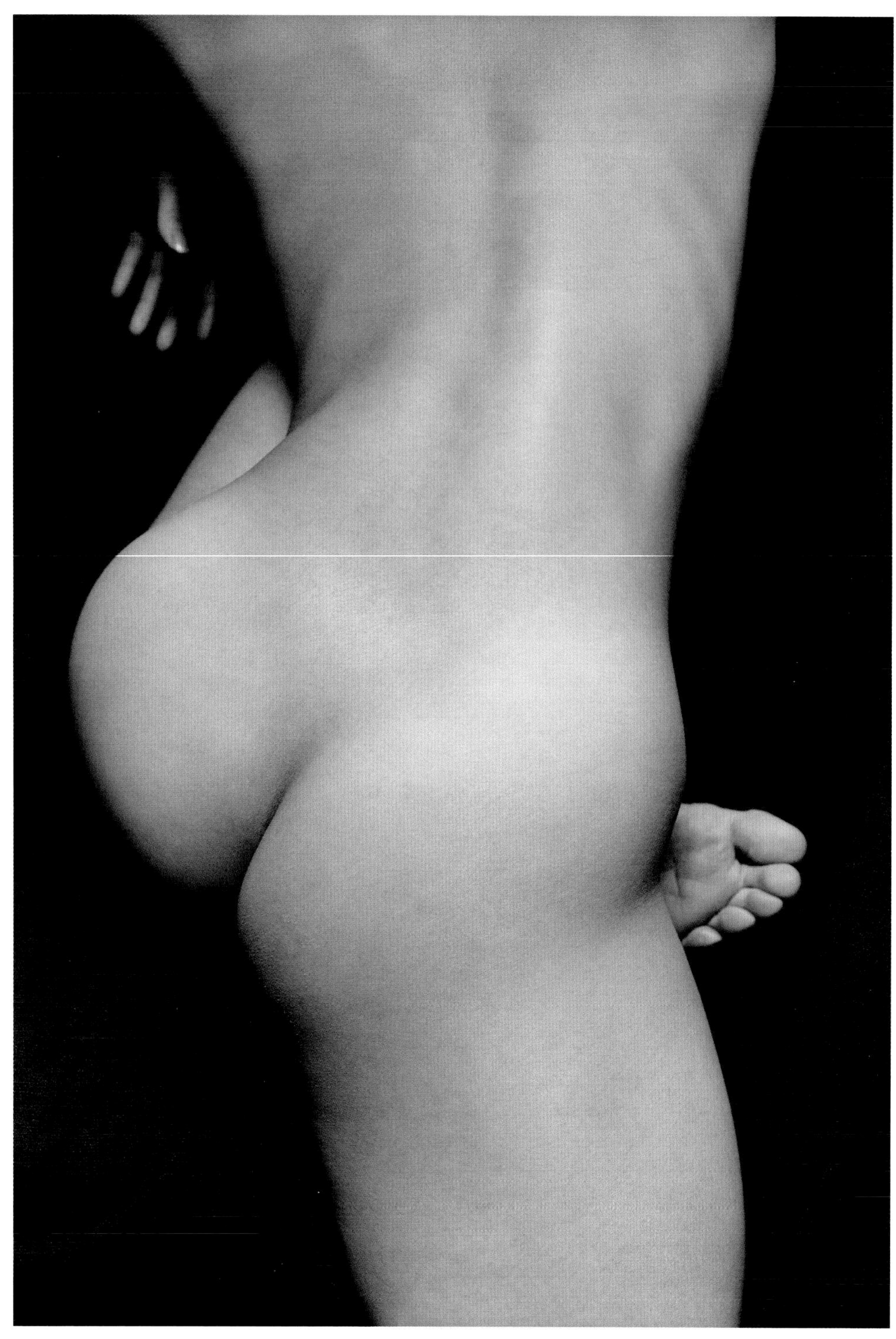

N-80, 1997

Wisdom Traditions

•

In the wisdom traditions of the East, there is the belief that art has the capacity to not only communicate *about* spiritual experience but to transmit those spiritual states. Even in our Western traditions, works of art are sometimes spoken of in terms of transcendence or illumination. The challenge of every medium, constrained by limitations, is to focus on the tangible in order to transmit the intangible.

When one views the photographs of Carl Austin Hyatt—whether a sensual nude or a luminous seascape—one is first struck by the impeccable and beautiful surfaces. The photographs evoke a palpable sense of desire. Hyatt knows desire and his images tingle with it. Linger a moment and allow yourself to be drawn deeper, past the surfaces and into an inner space. The foamy rush of ocean, the languid sigh of the model, the preternatural stillness of the standing stones or the whisper of the salt piles becomes real sound against the inner ear.

Hyatt's enigmatic images of standing stones seem suspended in a timeless moment. They can be seen as a metaphor for the viewer gazing at the photograph. Caught and transfixed by desire, seeing becomes meditation. The distinction between observer and observed begins to melt. Boundaries dissolve. Form surrenders to consciousness. We are, as William Blake said, seeing *"...a world in a grain of sand, and heaven in a wild flower."*

Hyatt's work has that Zen-like reverence for space and emptiness that, in the Japanese tradition, invites the Kami or the spirits to be present. His images not only allow this experience, they encourage it. Since he has been there before you, it's as if you can feel him there, holding the door open.

These images do not insist on a spiritual interpretation. They are the masterful artifacts of a photographer's quest to see. Yet they are something more. They could easily share space with the most sacred mirrors of spiritual art. In Hyatt's nudes, the feminine form flows like the brushwork of the finest Zen calligraphers—dissolving fullness into emptiness. His seascapes and salt piles contain all the aspects of divinity—contemporary yantras fully expressing the most sacred geometry. His standing stones have the stark simplicity of the most elegant Taoist watercolors. In his portraits, the erotic and the cataclysmic collude like the most sublime Tibetan thangkas.

These images suggest a way of being in relationship with the world. They are elegant pointing out instructions offering the real possibility of waking up *into* the world, the moment, the now.

—Tom Crockett, M.F.A., Rev.
Author of *Stone Age Wisdom* and *The Artist Inside*

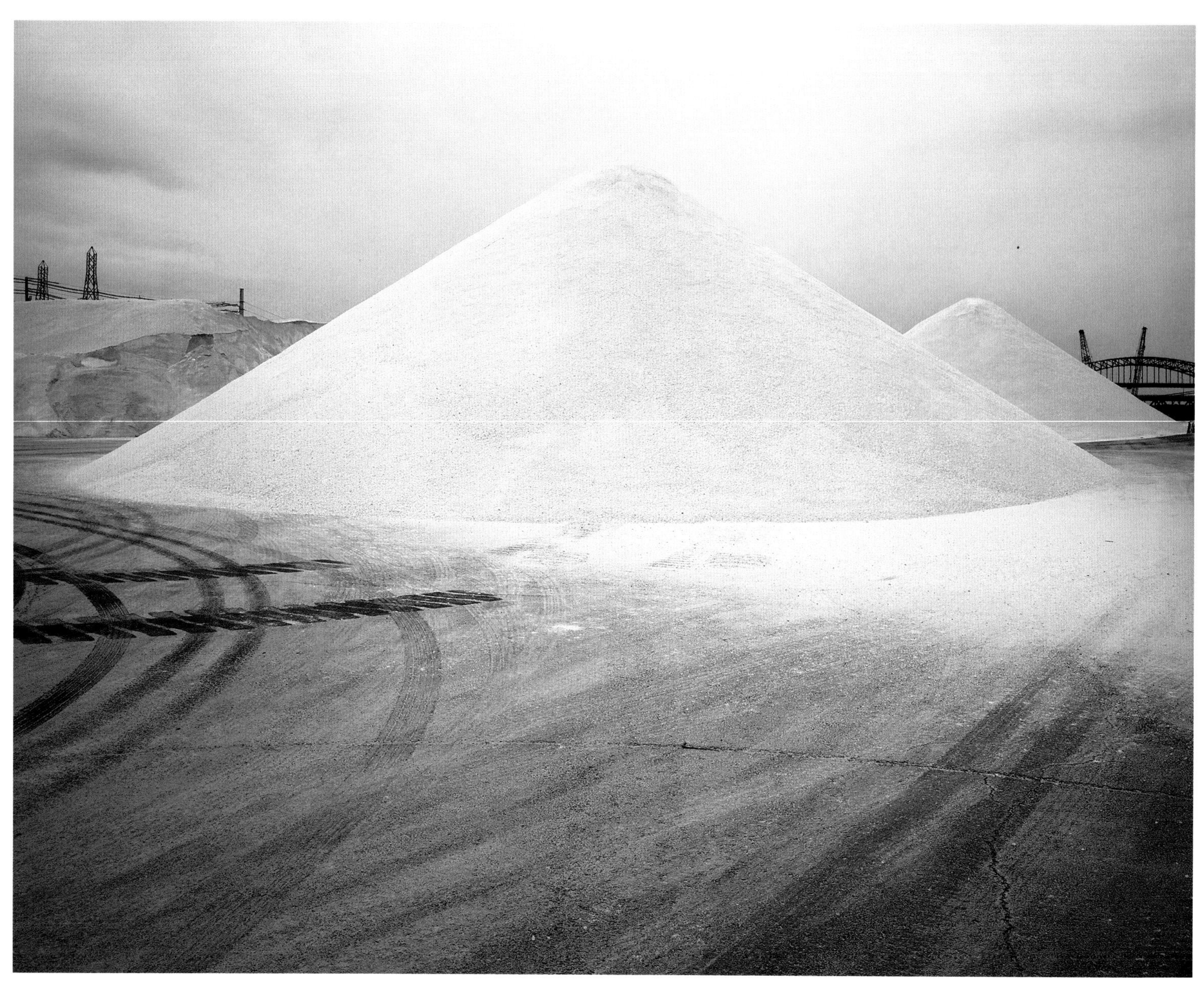

Portsmouth Harbor Salt Pile Series, S-16, 1992

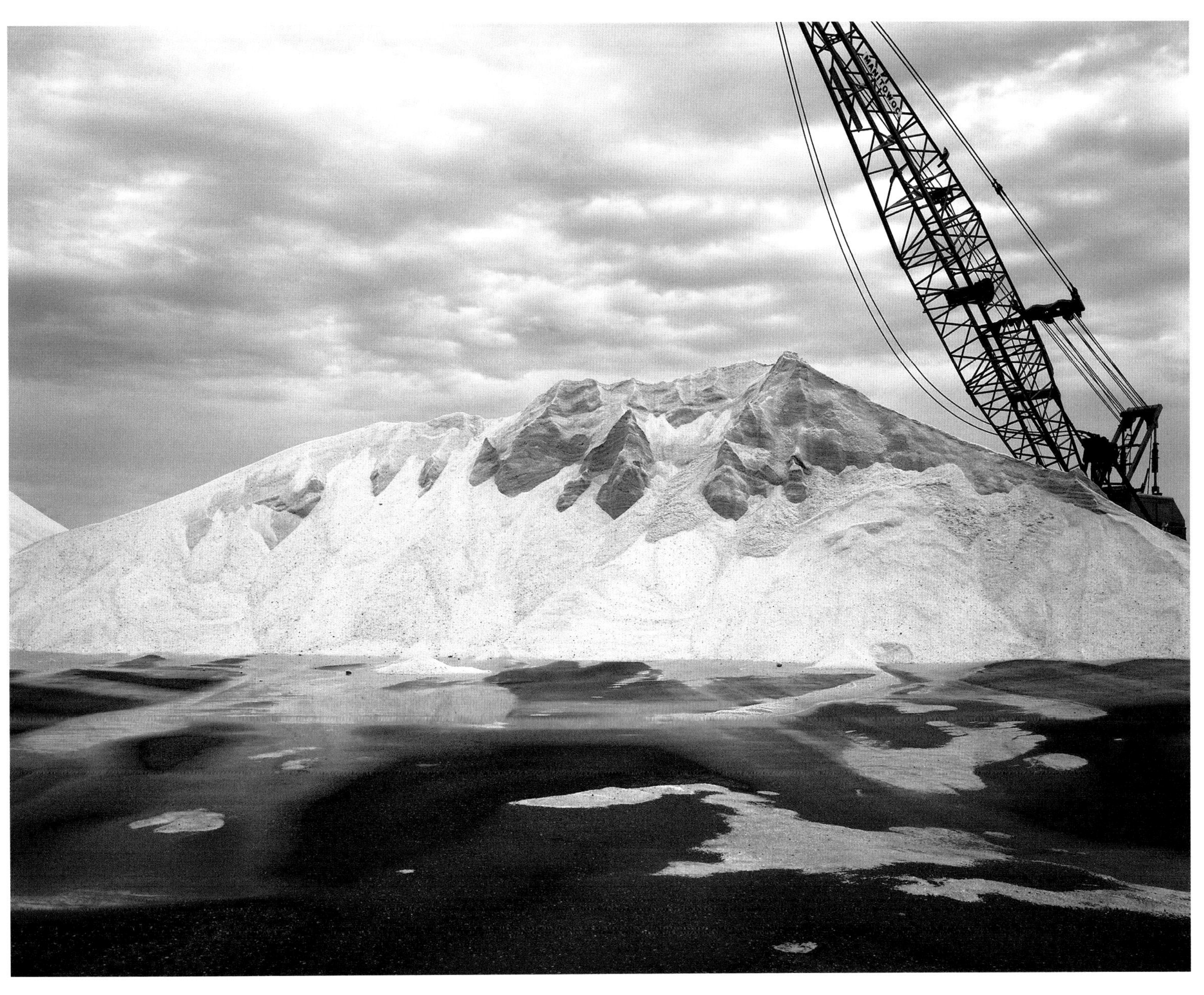

Portsmouth Harbor Salt Pile Series, S-27, 1992

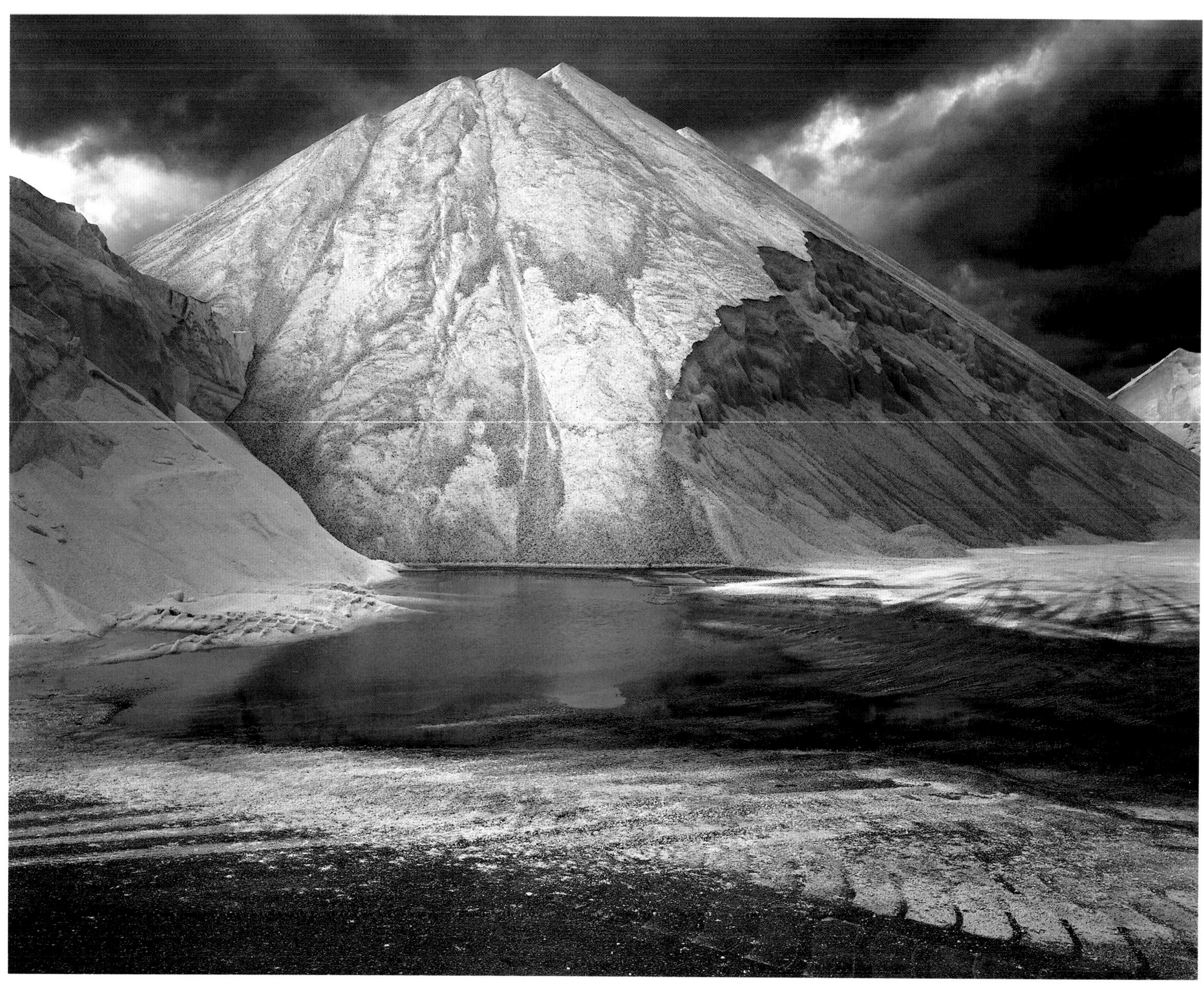

Portsmouth Harbor Salt Pile Series, S-14, 1992

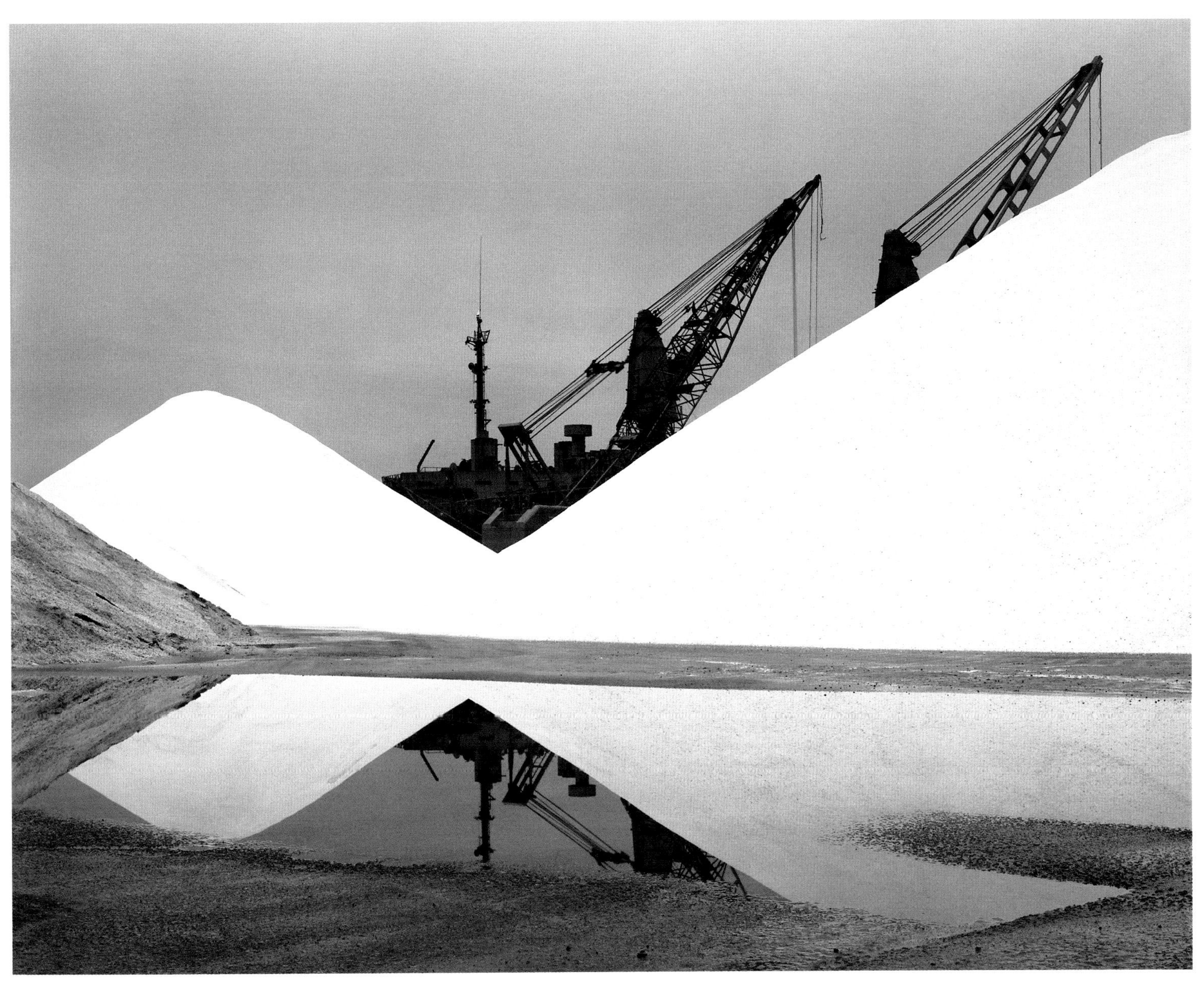

Portsmouth Harbor Salt Pile Series, S-28, 1992

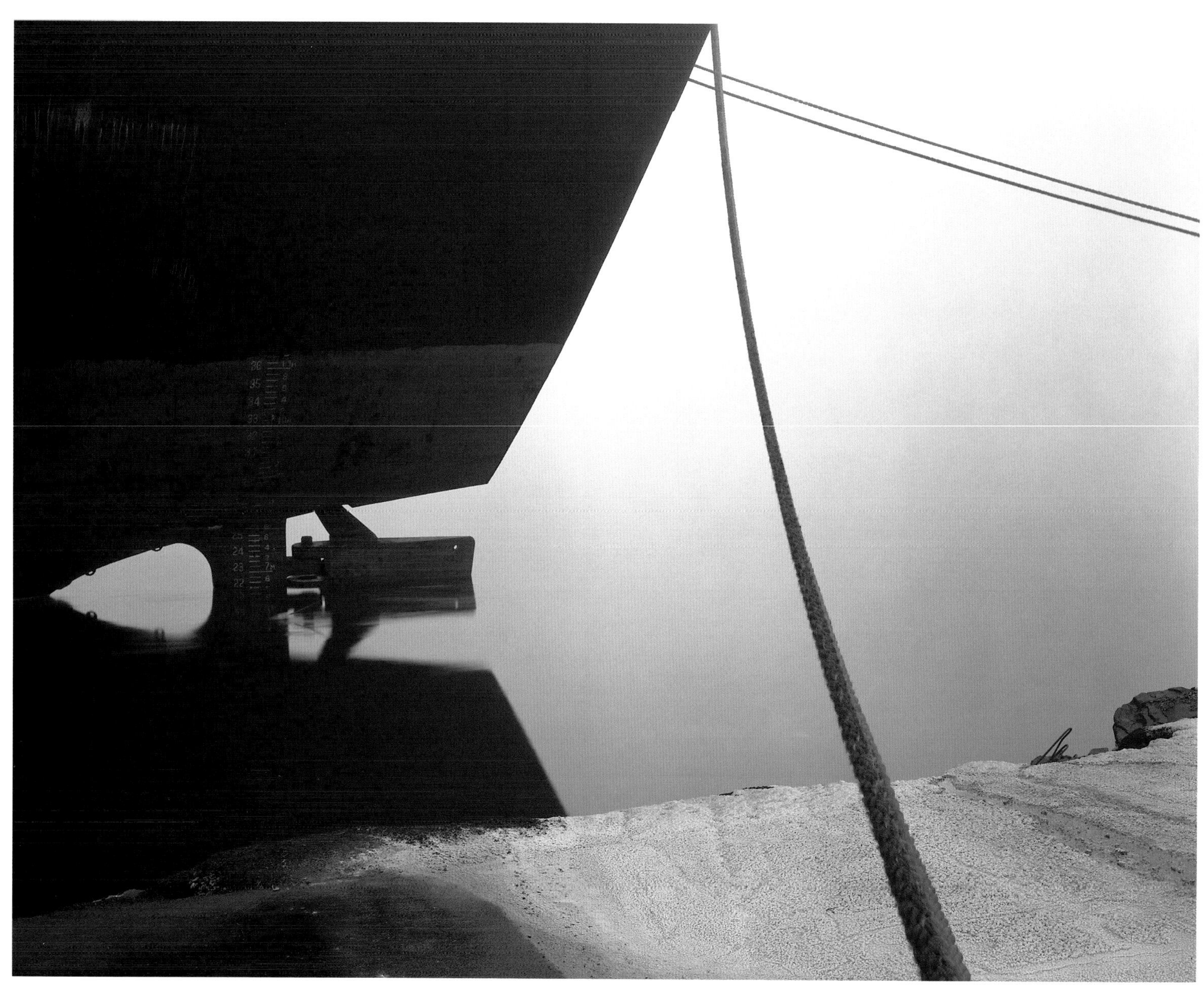

Portsmouth Harbor Salt Pile Series, S-12, 1989

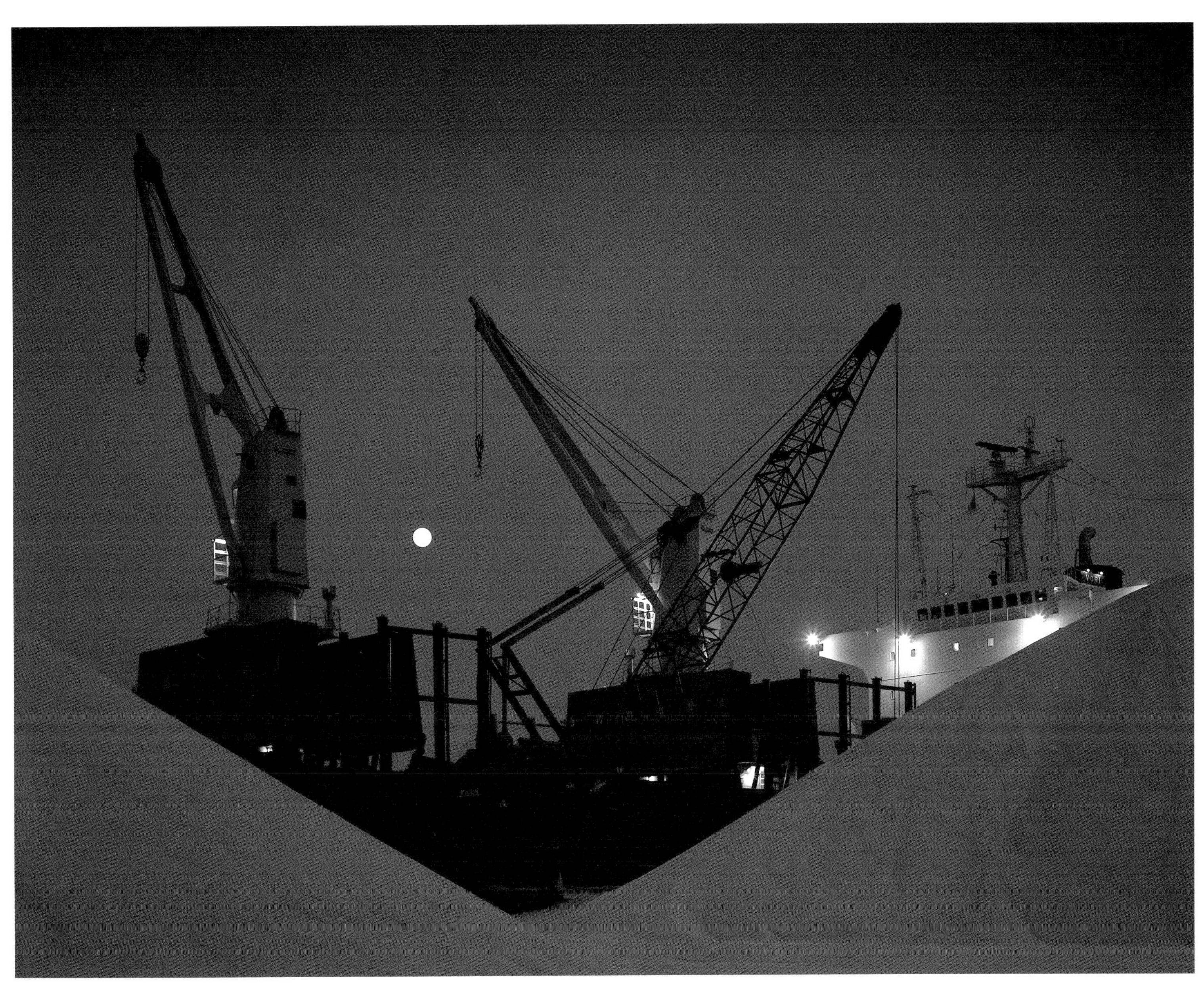

Portsmouth Harbor Salt Pile Series, S-25, 1992

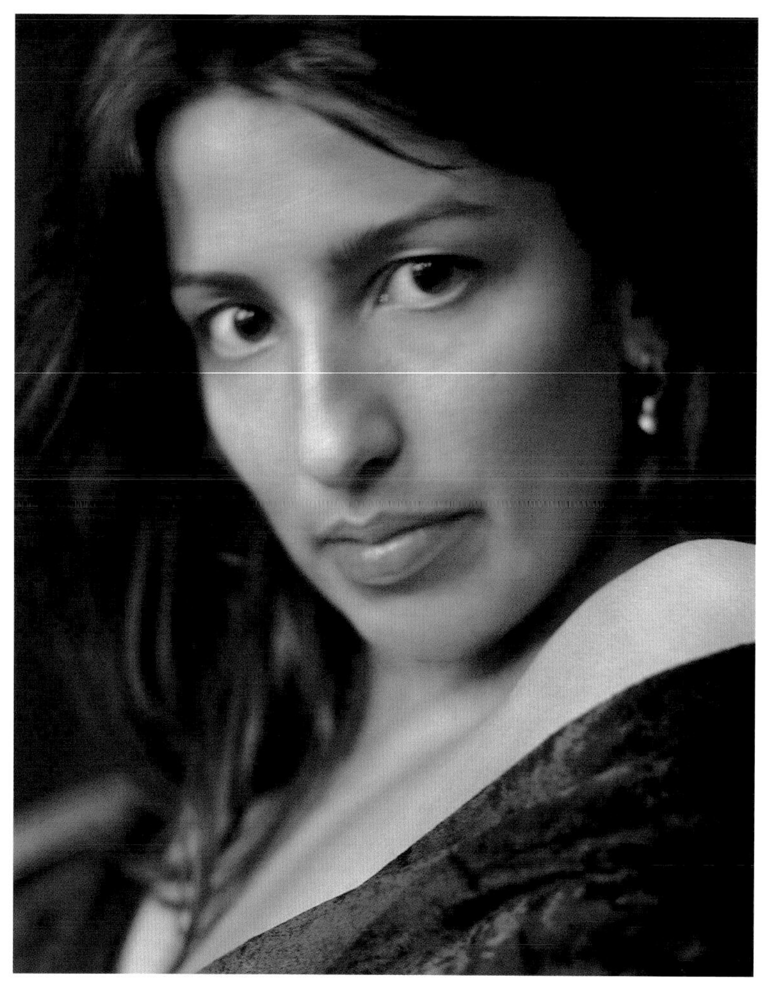

N-67, 1996

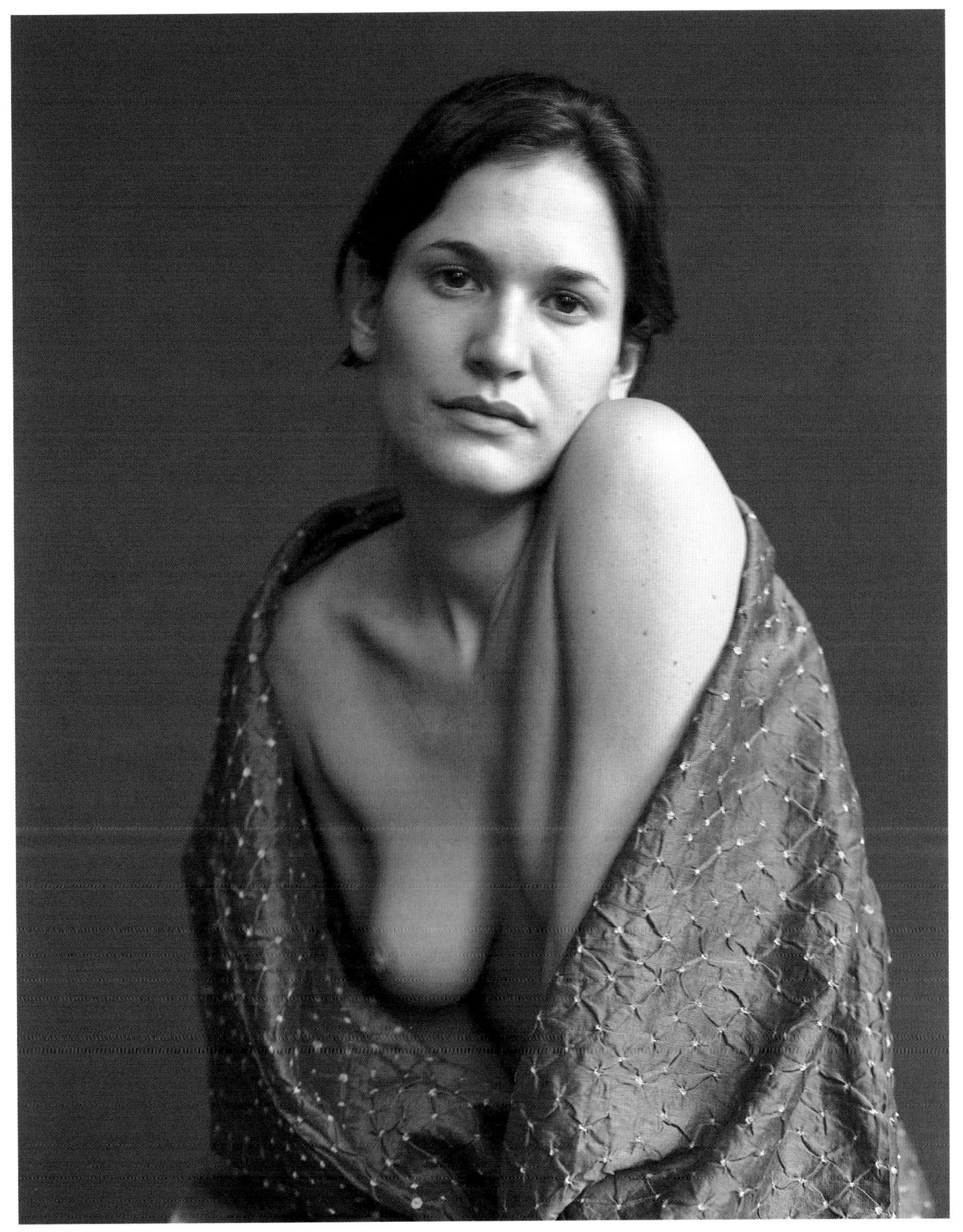

N-144, 2001

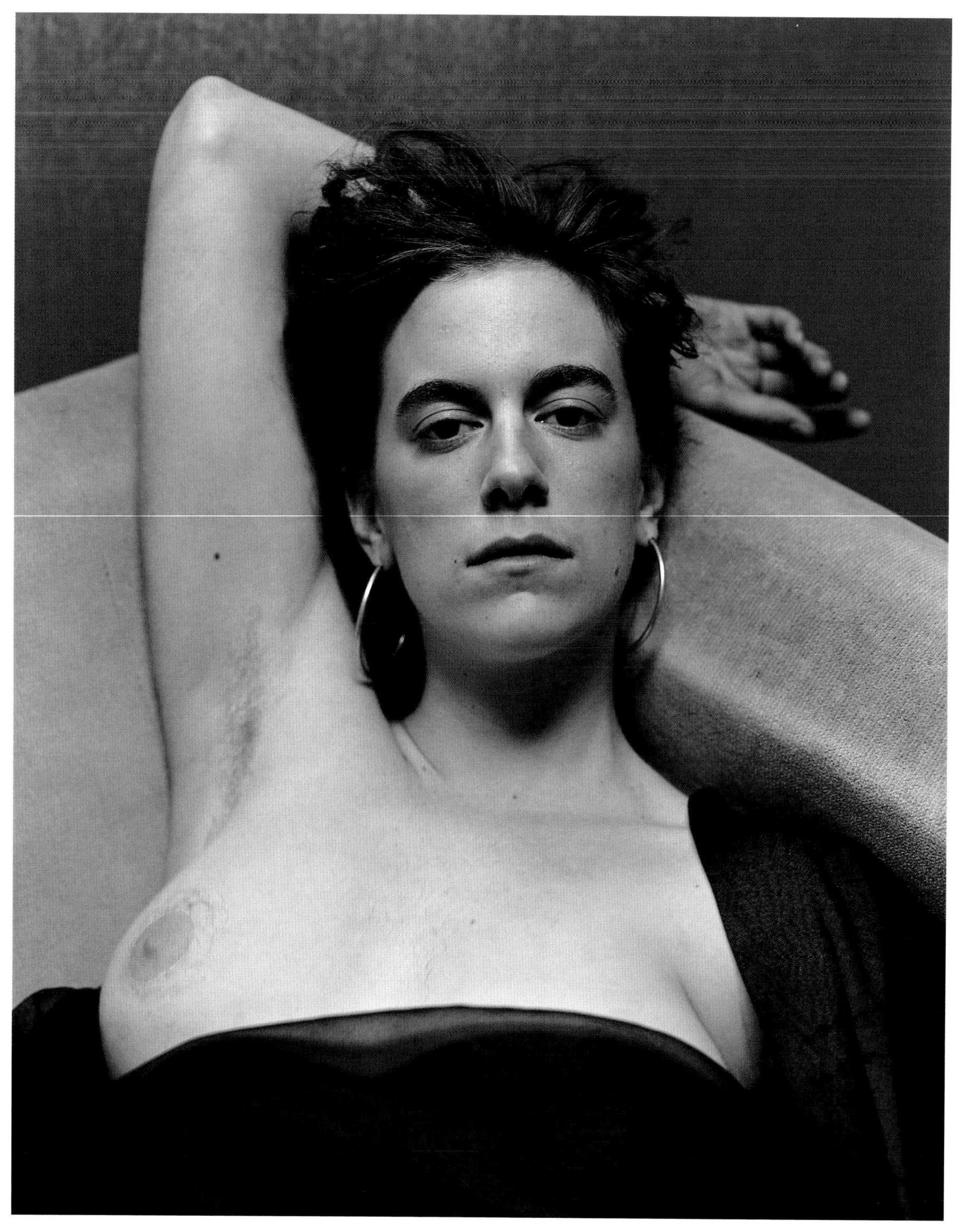

N-120, 1997

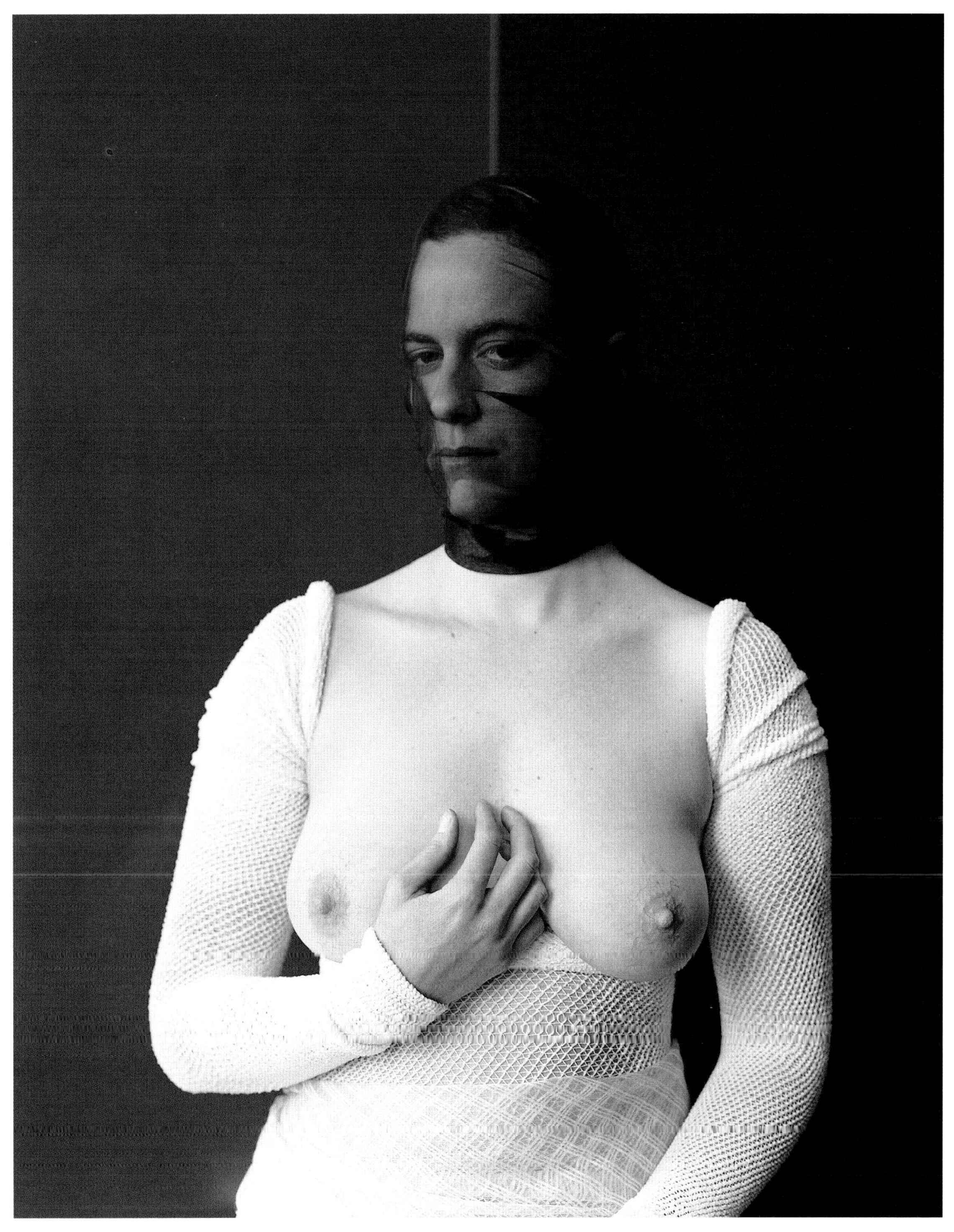

N-150, 1997

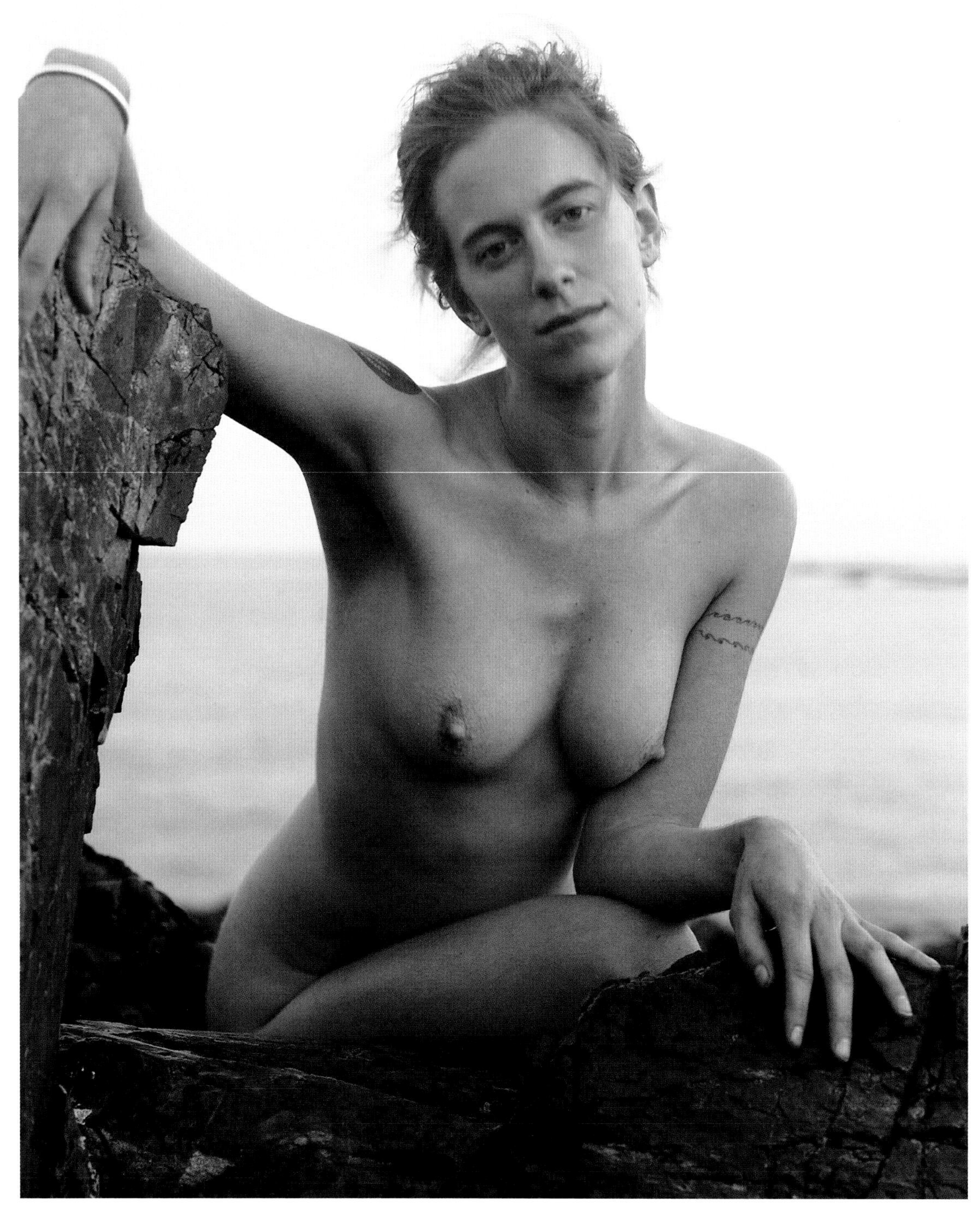

N-127, 1997

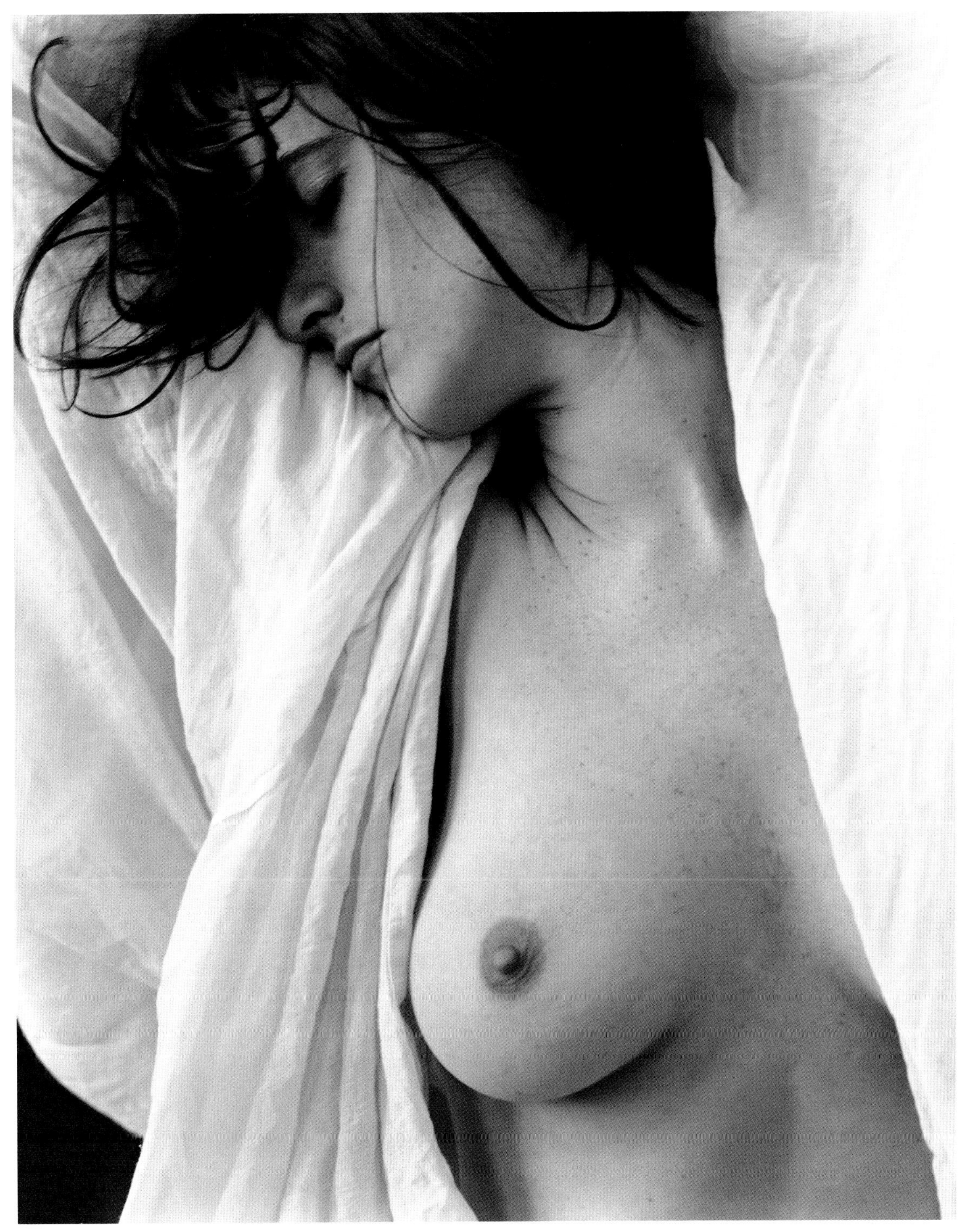

N-142, 2004

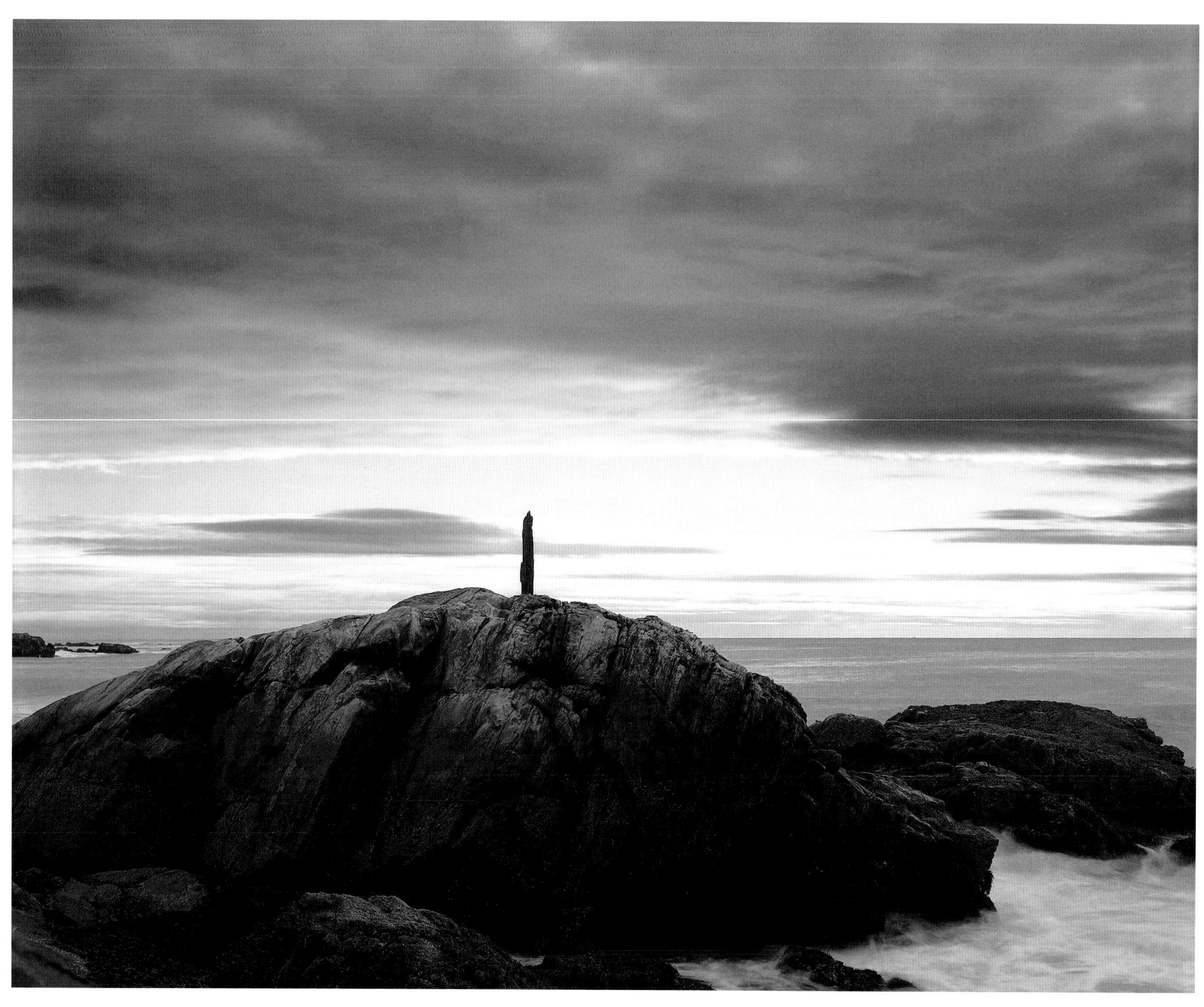

Standing Stone #3, 1994

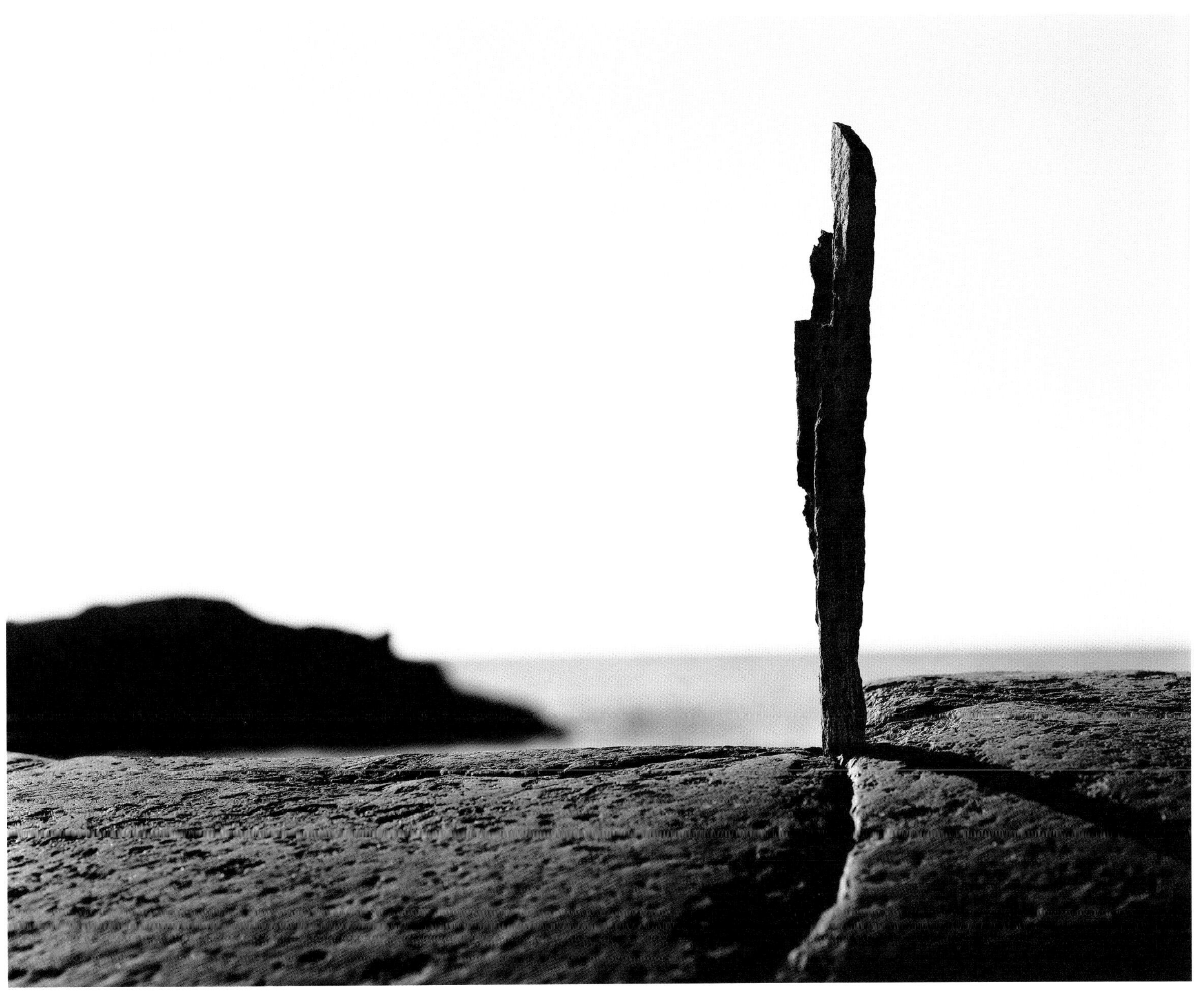

Standing Stone #1, 1993

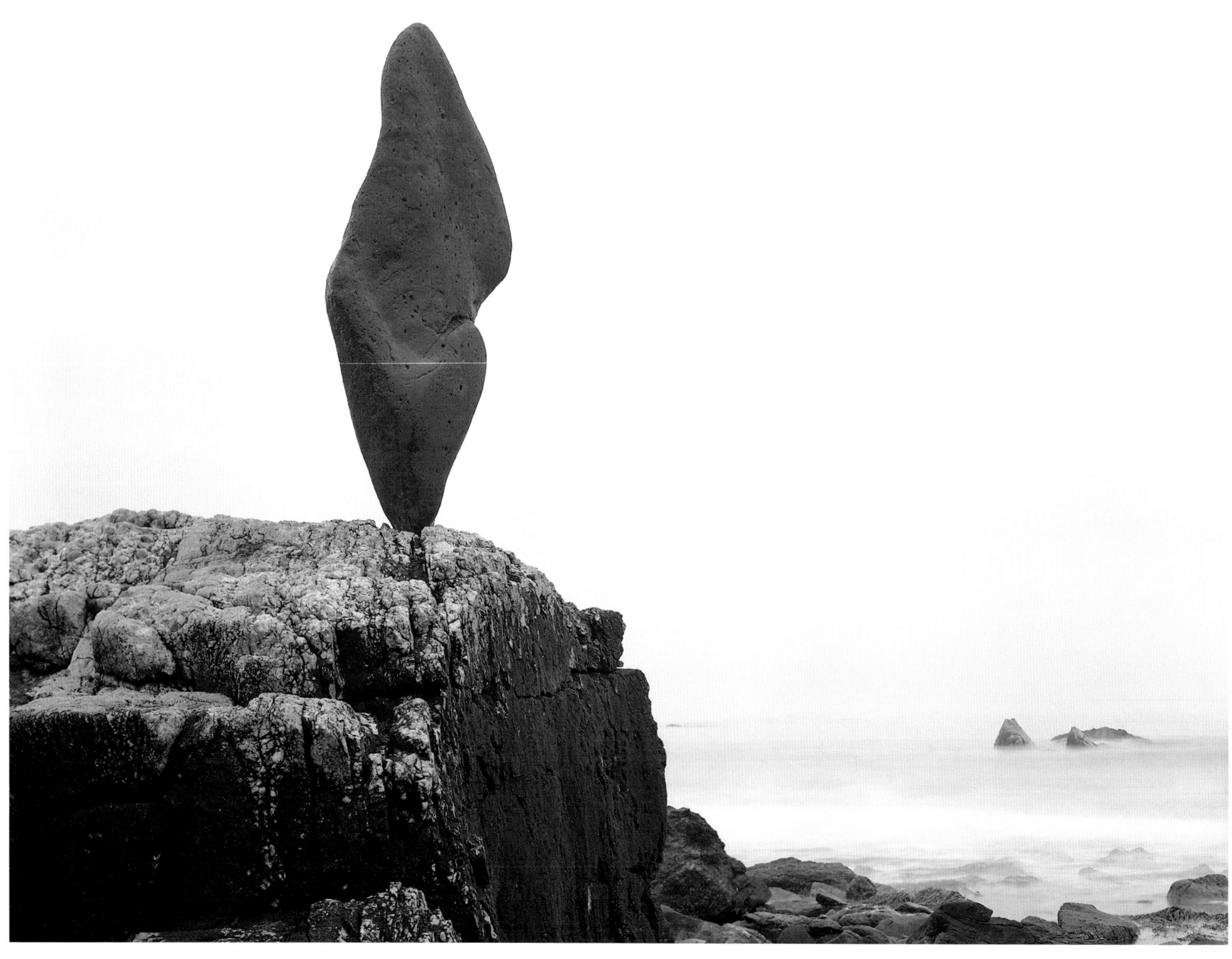

Standing Stone #8, 1993

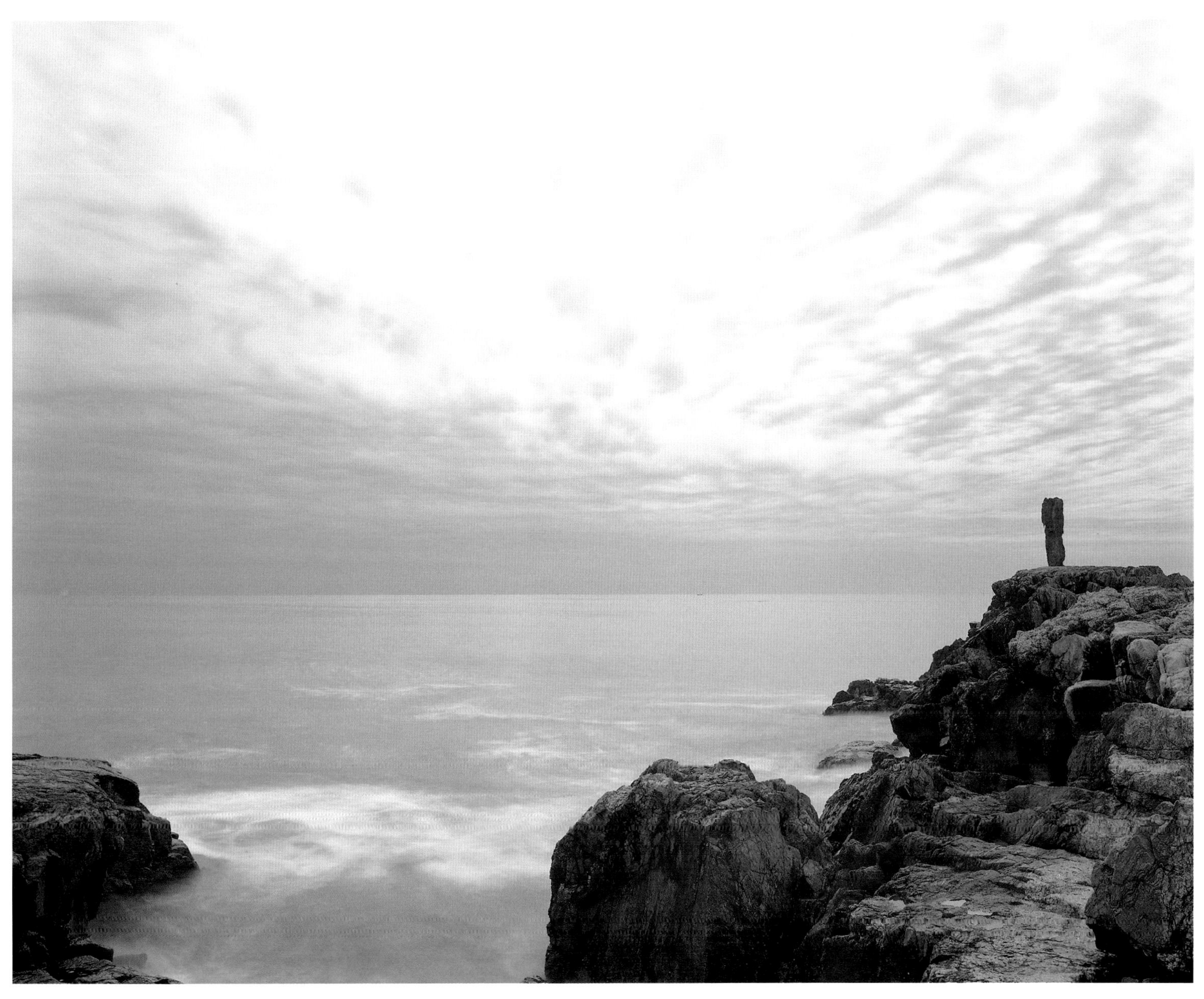

Standing Stone #5, 1993

Index